Voices II

An anthology of writings, images and musics
from the
North Cork / South Limerick frequency.

Charleville Print Collective

ISBN 0-9544741-0-4
Published by Limerick Praxis Press
Printed by: Carraig Print, Carrigtwohill, Co. Cork.

"Listen. Listen to the silence behind the noise. Do you hear it? That's the sound of possibility, of all the beautiful explosions of creation that are festering and waiting to happen, that are already occurring but we don't see them. Possibility scares some people, they are afraid of bad things, of a greater evil than is now known taking over. Fear not. Christ said that too. Fear not. Believe and hold the force of truth within you (satyagraha) and all the illusory figures of fear will fall from you, on your road to create peace and beauty in your life and the world." (Luther Blissett)

compiled by gerald fitzgibbon.
edited by gerald fitzgibbon and Michael Murphy.
photographs by gerald fitzgibbon.

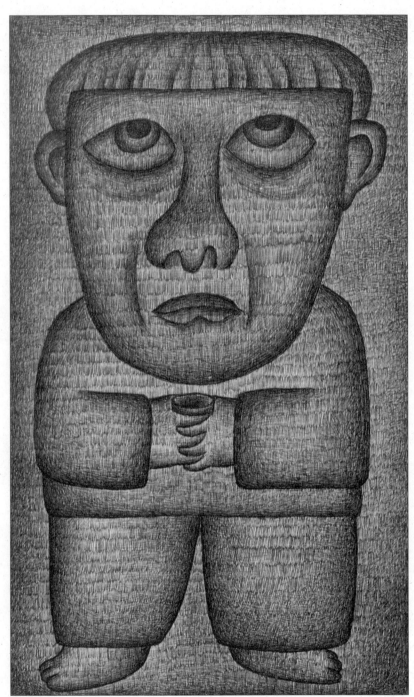

Drawing by Frank O'Sullivan

sort of an introduction

Irrelevant quotation: "We are what we repeatedly do. Excellence, then, is an act not a habit." *Aristotle.*

Some people build walls. Some people build books. This book and CD have no magical properties. The book is a humble and modest gathering of writings and images by people of or from Charleville and the surrounding landscape, North Cork and South Limerick, Ireland, Planet Earth, 2003 Human time.

Voices 1 was published in November 2000. The idea was to produce a different type of local publication, one that provided a space for the expressions/writings of people living now, that was inclusive and non-judgemental, that allowed people speak freely in whatever way they chose, with whatever words they chose.

That book was a modest success. It paid its printing costs and made a small profit, used to fund this publication. No follow up was planned, but material began to appear and it began to seem like a good idea to publish *Voices 2*. A loosely knit group called the Charleville Print Collective has come together to oversee the project. **Proceeds from the book will go to the locally based Chernobyl Orphanage Appeal, and to Children in Hospital Ireland (C.H.I.).**

The book comes with a CD compilation of local musics, an idea thrown out one night by a gentleman formerly of Tankardstown, Kilmallock. Like the other material, most of the music was already there, it was just a matter of tracking it down and drawing it together. The CD, a subjective sample with no doubt many glaring omissions, comprises very diverse recordings, from demos made over 20 years ago(the famous Dragster) to the very latest in raw young talent(Purgatory). In between are songs of tribute, snippets of jazz and traditional tunes and for the first time some of the long lost works of Ultrahoney, Moonboot and Bandog, 3 Limerick-based bands from the mid-to-late 1990s most of whose members were from the Charleville-Effin-Garrienderk-Kilmallock matrix.

Anyone with questions/suggestions about the book's form/content, wanting to post stuff on for a future edition, or generally needing to rant off, can send to **voicestwo@yahoo.ie** Thanks for the one email received about the last book!

Copies of the Voices 1 are still available for 10 euro (pp) from Maiden Hall, Kilmallock, Co. Limerick. **www.charlevilleprintcollective.org** is being made.

End of Functional Introduction.

Non-Functional Introduction Part 1: OK. A big thank you to all who, by entrusting their pieces to the editor(s), have allowed Voices 2 become what it is. Also a thank you to all those involved in the process of making this idea a reality. A thank you too to the various sponsors, thanks for helping this local initiative. Thanks to the air for allowing us to breathe it and to our food for allowing us to eat it, and to the process of evolution for allowing us minds and mouths to think and develop languages, eyes to see and fingers to type etc etc. Thanks also to the originator/cause/reason of this process.

Voices 1 was a difficult book. Both to publish and to sell. It contained a lot of dark material. "Here, buy this collection of local writings... it will depress you!" Not the best ever sales pitch. But it needed to be put out. The book was cathartic, it acknowledged a despondency that is real and needs to be addressed. That is good. Too often life in rural towns is about putting on the bravest face for those peering eyes that look and think they know. Why is everybody afraid to express emotion?

This book, Voices 2 is both very different and similar. It contains more a diversity of people and concerns, and the general tone is more positive. There is much to be celebrated, after all. A similar ethos of inclusivity applies. Nobody who submitted writings/drawings/photos/music was excluded. Again, this Voices is not an Art book, nor a Poetry book(though it contains much art and poetry). It's aim is not to make the national literary scene. (The material would fail for not being bland/tame enough)The book is made to engage our lives and thoughts in the here and now

This book continues to value and elevate this place and community, here and now. Of course people come and go, values change, the cements/chains of old community life (for better and for worse) are eroded. One wonders how much community really exists here today. Well then, let this book be part of us finding out where we are at, as we bring these voices out into the open air to hear what they are saying, here and now. Maybe the time has arrived for us to look around our communities, to see what their future might be, with openness, understanding and activism replacing obedience, obligation and passivity.

This book is an attempt to embody, in its form and attitude, the ideals of openness and acceptance of each other's differences and of continual questioning of ourselves and our surroundings. This book is a virtual space in which there are none of the taboos we encounter in local life, where we all think we know so much about each other's business... but where mostly we know very little: our masks get better each day, or else we flip out. Here are fitters, secretaries, barmen, mechanics, PhD students, housewives, mothers, engineers, drummers, nuns, priests, businessmen, journalists, solicitors, farmers, social workers, painters, poets, unemployed people, unemployable people, retired people, writers, rockers, rollers, school goers, college goers, healers, wheelers and dealers all expressing themselves unselfconsciously without mind or ego games or

4

any sense of being constricted by artificial social conventions. There is something to interest, humour, enrage, annoy, and enlighten everyone. This book is a virtual pub where everyone is guaranteed a drink, but where the only thing on the menu are the soul-mind-heart essences of each other's lives and thoughts and art. Come and drink.

Non-Functional Introduction Part 2: Human civilisation is undergoing massive changes all over the world, which now through developments in communications is a very small place. We each have our destiny, as individuals, there is also our collective destiny, as Homo sapiens. Human consciousness is also at a crossroads. Either we lose ourselves in the intricacies of our own self-made systems and realities(self-destructing in wars) or else we open our minds to the natural world on which we evolved, engage with the infinite expanse of universe which surrounds us.

Today is a good time to live in this country. For the first time in many generations, young Irish people have the choice of not emigrating, they keep with them their hopes and their dreams, along with all the hopes and dreams brought to these shores by the many foreign workers, refugees, asylum-seekers and students. The time is ripe for a flowering. For that flowering to occur we must have to courage to externalise our inner motions towards creativity and positivity, paying no heed to the cynics, and the knockers, and the gombeen men in our minds. Consumerist reality is just too soulless and boring for the celtic spark that burns within us. The weekly collective mass intoxication that we call Irish pub "culture" is a joke. Where else in the world would rampant alcoholism be called culture? We need to evolve new forms of social interaction. Otherwise Ireland will just have turned into a version of America without the hope and optimism. Muck savages in designer labels. What would Mick Collins have thought as he lay dying on the road? "Christ lads, I hope it was worth it." Should shoddiness and mediocrity become hallmarks of Irish culture?

It's a good time to live in this area. There are more economic opportunities and, of equal importance, two of the traditional reasons for not living here are gone. The gossips and the local Talibans no longer matter. Now we can live our own lives without taking flak from people who 'push fake morals insult and stare' as bob said. That's why this book exists, imagination creating space for something new to exist, or bringing what's already there out to the light. Beautiful. It's called Imaginaction. Imaginaction. Very nice. What's next?

Ok so, I've been waffling on for long enough now, the three pages of the introduction are filled. Let everyone do exactly what they want(so long as it doesn't detract from someone else's life experience).

Enjoy the book and CD, yours sincerely, Lalla-head/Emotional retard.

life

I have a dream to tell to you,
About a world, a world so new,
I have a dream, where I can see,
A wonderful place for you and me.

In my dream, all wars are ended,
All hate is gone, all fights are mended,
There is plenty of food to feed the poor,
It's a wonderful, wonderful world for sure.

People will remember to thank God above,
For our lives and all his love,
In my dream, my dream comes true,
It's a wonderful world for me and you.
(Mark Kennedy, age 12)

sharing some thoughts

Since having the choice of remaining unknown, I am sharing some thoughts with my country and county folk. Some have said "there's a book in you", but I'll settle for being in a book. While glancing through book 1, I could not help but pick up on the darkness and morbidity of the poetry. I have heard it in some music that I've heard in some live shows by hopeful amateurs in city pubs. Not being a musician or poet's critic, this is not meant in a 'better than thou' attitude. Being a bachelor by fate, this bit of a verse struck me after again clearing the sink; and since I had no hot water and used loose tea, this followed:

> He washed his weekly dishes
> With the scalding of a pot.
> He learned it in the past, he says
> For his parents taught him not.
> Maybe 'twas something he'd seen
> Somewhere along the way,
> Or heard some wise man talking once
> For the ear drums of the ......

Since fate again dropped me in the Hippy Era, a four lined poem summed up many years:

> I went looking for some flowers to wear,
> But I got entangled in my hair.
> What made my world into a snare!
> Took my smile and left a stare.

Giving a rough guess, this page would fit in a printed book page, so maybe I'll share this one:

> My fantasy's like a seed,
> Unable to germ.
> Like a being-born-chick
> As it hacks through the sperm
> Something had entered this little bird's brain
> When a 'peck' woke it up to the beauty of man.
> Electrical energies shone through a vein,
> Searing through blackness with pleasure and pain.
> Evolution. Evolving, as seen from within
> An image - a form - must be mother
> "Mummy" she cried, "get me out of this hell,
> I'm hungry, I'm thirsty, I'll die in this shell

My nature to suck - it seems but a dream
I ponder while waiting for peaches and cream.

'Twenty' long years for an innocent mind
nourished only by hope - to be one of some kind
My first steps to freedom - I trod very light
Some time on probation, please tell me my plight.

and finishing off with:
de se you coincidence - jigsaws so rare
a 'PIECE' was still missing - 'till a voice filled the air
'I am' now, the reason for your state of completion - why you've
lingered so long with your plight - your existing self - has been
long on the shelf - and - Darkness has won over light
(anon.)

christina's maze

Flickering sunbeam arrayed
Across a rocky stream river
Gazing upon its torrent green
Stems shiver. Mayfly tossed
In the gentle breeze. Wind
Among the clouds ascending out of sight.

Oak tree standing way out very high,
A colony of field fares
In the midst of the sky.
Fresh and green as the pasture
Where they're given repose.
Near restful waters out on the fold.

Perhaps a jaunt across the ford today
By the brow of a hill if I may.
Oh that rocky stream river,
Gazing upon its torrent
Green stems shiver.
(anon.)

the hand of little b sox

The hand that once filled this glove
Once clasped around mine
A small slender elegant sallow-skinned hand
Angelic angelica gentle sweet soft fingers
Her eyes a deep warm gorgeous brown
So much so
When I first kissed her
I sunk deep into her soul
And collapsed unto my knees
We once kissed for forty-five minutes straight
On Dublin's O'Connell Street outside the Gresham
Only breaking for air
As the sun broke the clouds
Awe struck as a heavenly garden blossomed out of the concrete
Enveloping our souls with all the essences of pure love
I disappeared deep into her gorgeous warm deep brown eyes
Anaesthetized by her sweet mouth and her gently clutching arms
She carved her lovely soul deep into my heart
Extended throughout the universe and into eternity
Time dissolved into infinite moments of perfect affection
But we broke up like the sorrow that follows a tragic death
Sometimes I think of her in loss with bitterness
Sometimes I hurt when I think of the hurt I caused her
But recently I think of her an amazing soul
Full of cleansing light
Not too unlike me occasionally climbing out of the wreckage of a broken
childhood
Trying to secure her spirit in an often cold and discompassionate world
The most beautiful woman ever I lived
the misfortune and heartache of break up with
(anon.)

scribble

Transform dross into diamond.
Invest ignorance with insight.
Cut cobwebs with consciousness.
Explode staleness with bombs of spontaneity.

Don't yawn with boredom,
Roar with life and energy.
Assault Stubborn Authority with Awareness,
And kill Cold Hearts with Love.
(anon.)

a relationship

Who was that naked man that crept in here and played with my heart?
What was the ritual we made?
No gifts, no love, no softness -
Pounding moans and compliments were his offerings.
I was grateful.
I took them as if he were giving me his heart,
If he had paid me, that would be more use.
(anon.)

(no title)

What comes in when love leaves,
casual chitchat and blazé farewells,
as if we never exploded at the exact moment with love swelling our bodies.
(anon.)

isolation

This familiar room where I have wasted away is seeped in the memories, the memories of my life.

It is a womb to my loneliness, a hiding place in, a room whose stench of my experiences suffocates me.

I sit here with my crutches on hand and the comfort has immobilized my will, trapped me into regression.

I have surrounded myself with my past, allowed it to arrogantly strut into the now.

There is no present, a vanity protests that what I do and feel are fleeting things that must be endured and waited out.

When I begin to live, all this will be numbed into another memory in another room, though not so familiar or so pungent.

This soothing warmth intoxicates me and I know as before I will suppress the struggling me.

It is a plant I don't want to water but can't throw away. It will sit here until I live.

(anon.)

(no title)

I will not fall back on an old love,

I will not crave a lost and only vaguely imagined intimacy, which was beautiful once,

and then fell away without dignity revealing ugly neediness and lonely times.

(anon.)

(no title)

Scratching and pulling,
To take away the urge.
Slimy and hot it leaks out and the need leaves me for a moment.
Things to do when everyone is outside -
I am a hand, I am a thought, working frantically I know what comes I know what leaves-
Nothing wants to hold onto it, transience isn't a threat,
    an act of love before I sleep that passes away without regret.
(anon.)

casual comfort

A little warmth to fill the void - the gaping hole that isn't fillable,
crowded with images of what it was, things that are now lost but are
needed.
Could you let me fill it up, drink someone else's sweat, pour in their juice
to wipe away the tears.
Could you watch me groping for it hungrily taking whatever I can (some
kindness I'd expect from you)
You can fill me up, pump it in, just let me back into those days.
I'll close my eyes and be with you, delayed it could kill me.
(anon.)

unfinished

Everything was so perfect, it couldn't be kept.
No pickles to preserve, all was impossible but we couldn't see that - our
reality was separate,
Separate from logic, argument, reason - strong currents of emotion
overcame our minds - took us to a new country, full of all the things you
need, all the tickles you can stand.
You bring yourself away from the country as he pulls up his trousers, a
sneaky exit before the morning looks on our shame.
You take the shame while he's away but only when you know he's coming.
The day can't last forever even when you measure in minutes (though each
is painful and wears you out).
Wishing away the actual reality of what you are when he's away, loving
yourself completely when he's in your arms. Wanting to swap the realities
but being too unafraid.
(anon.)

(no title)

Unknown to the world, without screams, without struggles,
I was gently raped,
By an embarrassed man who wanted to come and spilt his spunk all over
me.
I lay there unmoved and unmoving - waiting for my chance to sleep,
disconnected and drowsy.
(anon.)

if

If I had one single wish, I'd go back to the moment I kissed you goodbye.
No matter how I try I can't live without you in my life.
Maybe you'll say you want me,
Maybe you'll say that you don't
Maybe we're sad it was over
But I can't let you go
I walk around trying to understand what is wrong
Why it happens like that
Tell me why it happens like that
Nothing left to lose without you
There is nothing.

little house of dreams

Little house of dreams
Everybody need house of dreams
Where you can dream your dreams
Everybody need house of dreams
Where happy you can be
Everybody need house of dreams
Where love can always meet
Everybody need house of dreams
Where love is all you need.

Little world of dreams
Always helps to live your life
In that little world of dreams
Living here little dream
In that little world of dreams
Broken hearts get fixed again
In that little world of dreams
Everything is very strange
In that little world of dreams
Everything is happiness
In that little world of dreams
There is no start and finish
O my little world of dreams
I miss you very much

alone

Its night and I'm alone
I'm looking at the stars in the sky
I remember the last few weeks
When we were happy
Very happy
Now you're sitting on the plane, going home and I'm alone.
It's night again and I'm alone
I'm looking for the stars in the sky
I remember the last few weeks
Do you remember the last few weeks....
  (Andis Bonstets)

oh brother

Soon it will be mother's day,
I feel sad and lonely in a way.
This time last year, you were here,
for a confirmation and christening
and there wasn't a fear.

Now as a family we are sad,
left to mourn our brother, husband and dad.
With your illness, some days you weren't well,
through the eye of a stranger, one could not tell.

An artist, an actor and wonderful poet,
you won an award, and didn't even know it,
gone were you, a free spirit at last,
I have mighty memories of times gone past.

As I write tears fall on ink,
tonight I might not sleep a wink,
thoughts of you keep flooding through,
Orwin, I thought the world of you.

childhood hi-jinks

When I was young I used to play
in Sheridan's laneway everyday,
Richard, Vivion, Derek and me,
playing in our world, until time for tea.

Cardboard boxes were houses then,
grass and stones, I often served ten,
out with the football, on with the game,
Snake Sheridan would appear, oh what a shame.

Three fast gossuns, a blond in tow,
shure up the street, they'd have to go,
to persecute 'Red John' and the 'Yank',
then to the river, "Who'd dare walk that plank?"

We built a raft, from the base of a cot,
then sailed the river Inny, nearly drowned the lot,
we even went skiing, at a mill one day,
sawdust for snow, and it the month of May.

Snow would fall on the garden of Eden,
on Cassidy's Hill, we'd be found till evening,
from the Grove to the Bridge
the length of a Dublin street
we'd slide home in coal bags,
with jumpers wrapped round our feet.

It's the millennium now, kids don't play like that,
they're on the mobile for a chat;
them were the days you know,
when you'd just let the imagination flow,
we didn't think we were in Ballyjamesduff,
but we were, - and made of Great Stuff.
(Brenda Moynagh Bowles)

the mystical dawn

Out in the dawn, the night sky shunted gently across space to soft daylight. The trim elegance of a half-circled moon fading, leaving a shadow etched out in the sky.

Signs of the toil the night took on are on each blade of grass bowed over with moisture. It was parched from the sun.

Cast out between leaves is a web of wonder, dewdrops dangling like jewels left by the night that has gone forever.

And the sun is beckoning a new day over the horizon in masses of colour.

A symbolic stillness eases my spirit. There are no humans rushing. They are all sleeping.

I hear the cows as they pull the grass from just above its roots with one swirl of their tongues.

And the small calf gurgling and suckling from mother while she chews her cud.

Then a pheasant rises and graces the sky of the dawn - the mystical dawn.

Andis Beaslets

homecoming

As the train pulled into the station I rose to my feet. A crackly voice announced the arrival of the boat train on Platform Three. I was trembling with anticipation. I began to round up my belongings. I had a medium sized brown suitcase with two rusty hinges and two rusty locks to match.

It was my Da's case. One of his prized possessions. It sat on top of his wardrobe. Inside he kept the deeds of the cottage he had inherited from his father and a photo of his brother dressed in an army uniform. He left Ireland before I was born. He had a photo of mother and himself on their wedding day and their marriage cert. There was a brown envelope containing a golden curl. On the outside he had written: Nellie's Curl.

He had three pocket watches that no longer worked, a lot of old springs for clocks and his new cap wrapped in soft brown paper. It was a present from one of the boys and he only wore it on very special occasions, such as Christmas or Easter; or when one of the family was returning home from England for a holiday.

I laid my hand on the suitcase for a brief moment and paused. Then I yanked my duffle bag that was tightly wedged in the luggage compartment over my head, down onto the table. I pulled tightly on its cords and threw it over my shoulder. Thankfully it was a dry day so I did not have to worry about the contents getting wet. I had a creamy yellow paper carrier with big bold brown lettering. It read Martin Ford's Ladies Fashions, Kilburn High Road on both sides. I had been very careful throughout the journey not to crease this bag.

It had sat on the table in the train and when the stern faced lady opposite me looked as though she was going to give me another sermon on young people these days, I had slid down in my seat. I pretended I was interested in something that whizzed past the window and sheltered from her glare behind my Martin Ford bag.

This bag was meant to give me a sense of importance. I was a young woman now returning from London for the first time. It gave me a sense of self-confidence too, and I would make sure as I carried it, it could be read easily.

The other passengers and I edged our way along the narrow aisle in the carriage. I fixed my scarf around my neck and draped it across my chest before zipping up my red anorak. I tucked my gloves under the sleeves to keep out the sharp March wind that whipped our faces as we alighted from the train.

My body shook from head to toe with excitement as I was swept into the happy atmosphere that filled the platform. I made my way to the exit; there my eyes fell on a woman dressed in a black shawl. She was hugging her daughter.

Then my own mind played an unforgivable trick on me for in that moment I thought it was Mother. I had forgotten she was dead. I dropped my luggage on the platform as a fierce pain of sadness, or was it anger, gripped at the pit of my stomach. A flood of mixed emotions was about to engulf me but I had no time for sentiment. I reached for my luggage and as I moved on, I swished my head with youthful arrogance. I was going home to my Da. Everything would be fine.

Outside a line of hackney cars waited. With half closed eyes I gulped in the beautiful fresh Irish air and I thanked my God I was home. And I would not be going back for I had purchased a one-way ticket.

The roar of the train engine faded into the distance as I clipped my way in my new stilettos to the crossroads where I was to meet the milk lorry for the last leg of my journey home. A steady flow of hackney cars streamed past me until they were all gone by.

Now there was a strange quietness about the place - no traffic and no people. The cord of my duffle bag dug into my bony shoulder and my arm ached from the weight of my suitcase. But the crossroad was in sight now. The prospect of relieving myself of my luggage gave me the energy to hurry my footsteps.

Flashes of home kept my mind occupied. I could see the snow-white cottage, the rose bush trained to grow in an arch over the small green gate, the busy yard where hens, ducks and turkeys shared their day. There were the two front windows dressed in white lacy nets and Lass lying at the front door.

I could see my Da busy around the house preparing for my homecoming. Surely he would have the deep blue tablecloth with the red roses, trimmed in white, on the table. Would he remember to take out the ivory handled knives and silver forks that were kept in a box wrapped in white tissue paper in the bottom cupboard of the dresser? They only saw daylight on occasions such as this.

He would most definitely have purchased ham, tomatoes and Keating's sliced pan. He would have cold hard-boiled eggs and the kettle would be singing, ready for the tea. I could see him pacing the kitchen floor. I could smell the Mick McQuaid as he pulled on his pipe. I could see his blackened index finger he used to tamp the pipe as he reddened it. I wondered if he would like the fancy pipe I'd bought him. I hoped it would stay dry. 'We will go for a long walk after our feast,' I thought, 'and I'll tell him all the news about London.'

I was at the crossroads now. No need to look left or right. The road stretched long and empty on either side. I laid my luggage on the ground and massaged my shoulder with my gloved hand. The fingers of my right hand were numb so I removed my gloves to massage them. They looked flat and deformed from the weight of the case. I rubbed them back into shape. I slipped my two hands up my sleeves and held my arms close to my chest and hunched my shoulders up and down. I hopped from foot to foot.

The noise of the wind through my hood resembled far off thunder. I turned sideways to relieve my ears. Shortly the lorry appeared in the distance. I put on my gloves and picked up my luggage.

When the driver pulled up he jumped down from his seat and came round to help me. 'Welcome home, Kate,' he said, his hand outstretched.

He tried to fit the case in at my feet but the space was too small. 'You'll have to put it on your lap,' he said. 'Fire the old bag down at your feet.'

'Oh, God no. It's fine really. I'll rest it on the case.'

'Whatever you like yourself.' He returned to his seat and I fixed my Martin Ford bag on top of the case.

The journey home was pleasant and in no time at all our cottage was in sight. My heart was pounding now. I expected Da to be at the gate when we pulled up. But the door was closed and when no one appeared the driver left his seat again and I passed my duffle bag and suitcase to him. Then I jumped from the step of the lorry and thanked him.

'God be with you, girl,' he said. 'Sure it won't be the same for you now. It never is the same when the mother is gone.

I dismissed his remarks and hurried excitedly across the road. The white wall that surrounded the house looked grey and tired and spotted with a green fungus. The little garden on either side of the path showed signs of neglect too. The patches of visible soil were hard and crusted. Only a few bunches of daffodils grew here and there.

Lass was not at the front door. The hens were making a great racket. The cock that was sidestepping around a hen, stopped, stuck out his neck and began crowing. Lass lay in a comfortable bed of straw between the shafts of the cart. A duck waddled hurriedly from the wall outside the big gate, quacking. There was no sign of turkeys.

Poor Lass was on her feet now, wagging her tail, her lovely face alight. 'I'll be out to you in a few minutes, Lass,' I called to her. 'I must find Da first.'

I let down my case and opened the door. A stream of sunlight shot across the kitchen and settled on the back wall. A stale smell, combined with soot, filled my nostrils.

Da was sitting in mother's chair by the side of the range that was covered with inches of ash and turf bruss. He looked like a sweep.

'Da?' Only a faint whisper fell from my lips. He looked bleak and empty. I started to make my way across the kitchen to hug him. Suddenly I felt as though something was holding me back. My excitement, the rustle of my anorak, my whole being became amplified.

I stood, numbed with sadness. I felt as though I was an imposition on his bleakness. Tears streamed down my face and blurred my vision.

'Da! Da!' I said. 'It's me, Kate.'

(Kathleen Boyd)

The Cut 29 - remember the day mother on Monettia Bog

Remember the day mother on Monettia Bog
Your hair a mass of bog cotton seed
Our bog plot not a stone's throw away now
From your grave in Cluain na Slí

The whole party of us were up at dawn
Dressed in our oldest duds
That another turf stain wouldn't matter

We piled into the cart-like motor car
Eight loaves made up into sandwich shapes
Fish juice ebbing forth like blood
For our Friday lunch later on

The horse was bailed all night
In ready for journey
As soon as he found the track of soft earth
Half his work was done

He unloaded us
To the flat as pancake ground
Letting us get on with the cutting

He tasted the bog myrtle
And a clump of fox gloves
But spat them out as quick

You mentioned that you could see
The graveyard at Cluain na Slí
From our bog plot

Only years later
When I no longer drew in turf
Or bailed hay
As silage for winter fodder
Did I remember how poignant
Your observation was

Mother today is your eighteen anniversary

And I stand on Monettia bog
Blowing kisses down on your Cluain na Slí grave
And the occasional weather vane
By the way
The turf's all been saved

The Cut 48 - my poems are small flames

My fires are as abstract as poems
First kindling gathered down by the lake
Under dead Dutch elm who leaves branches go diseased
Just right for twigs

Then into wood shed
Carry armful of assortments
Branch trunk twig
Laurel ash beech

Collect once old oak floorboard
For Castle Oliver ballroom
Giving an extra kick start

It's not long before
The flames are dancing
To the spitting

Then heat rises up
Like host to god
In unleavened bread

I'm off with quill in hand
Of ostrich feather
Dipped in inkwell

Dripping leaking alphabets
Onto lines of pages
In other incarnation tree

The Cut 38 - knockin' about 2

Other days I sized up the world
From a Fiat Bambino Uno with sunroof
My mother would get us to
Sing places into being

To distract herself from herself
The poorest reader in the car
Would be appointed
To read the road signs

Bellair Hill I'd shout
Or Pullagh
Timahoe
Agall Glebe
Cobblers Hill Cross
Badger Hill
Reary Valley of Clonygark
Togher Tober
The Cones

I loved the signs with animals in them

Berry Bog 1

We've been cutting the turf all day
Slicing it into thick clods
To feed bread to our fire in the cold
Slice by brown slice I'd hold
In the mouth of my arm known
As my hand and feed the grate to size

I'd measure the flicker
By the number of sods I'd thrown on
And watch how they fit the kettle

Singing a long slow tune or minute
By minute I'd peer in the pot
Measure the length and height

Of the bubbles enabling me to throw
The spuds on top of the sods
Or spaghetti dumped in the bolognese

For the nights
We're feeling exotic by our
Turf fire from Berry Bog

hide and seek in Berry Bog

I jumped between dents
Of the earth the home made-valleys
Dark brown the colour of bland
I imagined a run for cover

A bell of siren in yell get down
I would crouch my small body dwarf
Lie roaring laughing face down in the bog
Its smell as natural as fig in leaf

I hold stillness like the early morning
In Berry Bog wondering which delve my friend
Had occupied was she down full length
Stretched out coffin-like

Or was she all-fours for the ground
Arms as paws or just
On twos which drain or dyke
Was she poured into

Was it the one two dips
Away from mine or had
She ran far down the bog
Would the bogey bogman get her

Then I'd sunrise out of my
Punctured earth and run from bog
Hole to bog hole calling
Berry berry at last I'd catch
The rim of her head peeping
Caught

berrying in Berry Bog

Cuttin pickin savin all the same in Berry Bog
Tying your skirt up into a bow's
Knot won't be the first time you're
Dress held fruit in front

Plait that flaxen rope out your eyes
Be ahead of them staring straight
At the golden thornheads to avoid
Those thieves of blood vampires

Go straight for the flesh whether
Black or red make sure the
Shape is heart and round
Volumed to the split in bloodred juice

Empty a sampler in on top of your cement
Molars check the depth of their sweetness
Outcry a squelched eaten to the pulp
One in a spit of tartness worm

Never thought such sweetness in ditches
What a turkish delight sweetness

Bramble laden down in gravity fruit
Won't be long till the rain will sweep

It back over its ditch like a strand
Of hair I'll have lessened its load
The chosen one with blood seeping through the
Front of my dress in exoticness juice
Like menstruation
Busy berrying in Berry Bog

a poem of silver ashes
I've saved the bank
Deposited myself on top of the cart
In a red shawl to stop
Up the draughts

The whole way home
Each hill I climbed made
Made me call out from the
Child within

Each pebble I felt
Like princess and the pea
As the horsepower
Chucked me home

I constructed circle stacks
And triangular turf piles
To keep the boredom at bay
Of rectangle on top of rectangle

And when in winter nights
I could see
The moon floodlighting
My sculptured shapes

I'd smile and hurry
In with armful
Lighting big fires of
Poems for me to dream in

far-mer distant-sea 15 - a poem

Oh that a poem
Stood out like cow lick
Projecting lock of hair gold
Compact and clear as cow-pat
Flat round piece of dung
Shining like cow-hide
Of a leather whip shaping poem up
Nuances reeking like cow-parsley
With umbrels of flowers
Cascading in Queen Anne's lace
That the poem would yield meaning
Like cow-tree
Dripping a sap juice resembling cow-milk
From Venezuelan arbus of brosimum utile
(Déirdre Carr)

Photo by Deirdre Sheehan

(no title)

Blue and Pink bodies writhing together,
Sweating away the paint,
Licking the colours,
Uncovering our flesh,
Falling in love.

(no title)

In a room in Sweden there is a picture of my sister,
She doesn't know how many rooms she has followed me to,
She doesn't know how many more she will adorn,
She doesn't know that with her face she gives the room the hint of famil-
iarity that makes it mine.

breakfast

In love, out love and all around the world,
Take me, take you , maybe neither of us knew-
Giggling in a morning and reassured that smiling cannot be unlearned.

(no title)

From the subcontinent to the Northern lands,
A telepathic message arrived in my make- up bag -
Searching for tweezers, the tiger's eye untangled and told me it is his
birthday.

(no title)

Kama Sutra in a denim jacket
No one told you a witch from the west would steal your heart and thwart
your brain
Red rose, Pink rose, White rose blue,
I don't mean to do the things that I do,
I love your smile, I love your heart.
You give it to me and I didn't ask you to -
So is it my fault for taking it or yours for being too unafraid?
(Emma Carroll)

the ups and the downs

(i)the low

I sit on the edge of my chair in a dusty room staring at the fire.
There is nothing to eat but half a packet of liquorice allsorts, an apple and three teabags.
I spill washing powder on the apple.
While peeling the apple, I drop the knife behind the cooker.
I ring the Social Welfare Department about cheap burials.
I have a dull headache, but have finished the last of the Paracetamol.
I knock down the curtain rod, while watering the spider plant.
I return from "Zefirelli's" to find that my cardigan is up, and my skirt is down,
The tea is cold, so are the chips and there are cobwebs on the apple.
I ring Dr St Claire, at his chess tournament to tell him that I have Zachariah's Foot.
I go to bed.

(ii)the high

I write five love letters.
I have a face like Miss Piggy and a figure like Lana Turner.
I walk home from Middle Town.
I tell the curate the one about the bishop and the chorus girl.
        I ring the accountant to ask if there is a tax rebate on my over-
heads, such as high heels and black lace.
There is fragrance in the air.
I do the laundry, wash the floor, clean the windows and write a book -
Chapter 1.
I find a cure for HIV.
I raise the Siege of Orleans.
It is 2 am, and there is a motor bicyclist offering to make love to me through
the key-hole.

(iii)the day after

I delete the five love letters.
I apologise to the accountant.
I apologise to the curate for the joke about the Spanish Inquisition.
I apologise to the doctor for the one about Burke and Hare.
I apologise to everybody else that I can think of.
There is a twit on the phone trying to tell me about his mother.
I ask him if he's read "Hamlet".
I get phone number changed.
I'm exhausted.
No wonder this list is so short!

dolletté

I know her father is in heaven,
Her little doll is deep asleep;
It does not breathe, or share the darkness,
It cannot heed the starlight's peep.

In the night she dreams of dragons,
Lambent flame, of octopus,
Lamprey's grip and lips of serpent,
Dim, soul-seeking incubus.

Someday her doll looks up to morning,
Glinting gleams and rocks of age.
Twinkling glitter in the bough-tops,
Trickles through the foliage.

Shear away the leering shadows,
Still the troubled pulse of lust.
Silver spills of light in heaven;
Dragon-slaver bites the dust.

For yes, her father is Almighty.
I trust that He will show his face.
His seraphim will burn in ardour,
And she will sleep and dream in grace.

felling the tree

Buds blossom, rain softly. May!
You grow lissom and true in your branches.
Summer is somewhere for me.
Let's ask for a truce, whisper softly;
Pretend it's for ever, yes,
May it be still our endeavour,
To root ourselves here in be-leaf.

Too frail for your leaves falling lost is my combing,
Too meagre my smiles to re-dress you.
Yet, today I'll be fast. No more roaming for me!
Let them sever perhaps.
We shall see dust together, be lapped -
Not in worm - but firm wood, in warm blood,
In warm arms, in warm wood!
(17 April 2002)

persephone

Persephone is the daughter of Zeus, queen of the dead, and wife of Hades. She spends spring and summer on earth, returning to the underworld each winter.

I leave my grave lord on the staircase,
To the limp, grey wraiths of the lost.
I hem my dress in a mantle of mist,
I am the darkness under the dust.

The sunbeams exult in a shower of stars,
The flower yields its stem to be plucked.
I am the thorn on the rose;
Where moss creeps, I am the rock.

I shall linger till gold turns to amber,
And the swans wing the air as they sail,
When the ash of the sunlight is silver,
And the gaze of the dawn is a veil.

I am the bones of the quercus,
The shudder bedewing the air,
The green palm frond in the catacomb,
The tear on the candle of yesteryear.

In the shadows of Hades I kindle the tapers.
My lord holds my fingers in his stern palm,
With his cold breath he chills my fair skin.
The night is long - a night without morn.

I seek the thin souls in the cellars,
Those who are lost to the truth.
I tell them my Father will free them.
I temper the scales with the petals of ruth.

I tell them that He will show pity,
For our Father is lord of Elysium.
The sword of His honour keeps the city,
And Psyche's roses will rise with Proserpine.

the calendar

The child was feeling peevish; her brothers were calling her: Silly, Silly! Usually they weren't allowed to tease her as it was two against one, but it was the day after Christmas; there was a snowy rain and she couldn't go out to play with Pip. Her mother was stirring gravy, her father was stirring a headache cure and the boys were fastened to the video game.

She was Sylvia because her father had been lucky with an outsider the day after she was born.
Her Grandma sympathised with her mostly: "What kind of man calls his daughter after a horse?"
    "Mother, please don't complain - the favourite was Casino Gal."

Sylvia was cross, but she wasn't tempted to go out without telling anybody, for her father was truly awesome when he was displeased. She was thinking of "Home Alone" - If only her family would disappear for a while, so that she could have the playroom to herself! However - perhaps she couldn't make them vanish, but she herself could escape for a while. She slipped out of the kitchen and into her father's study.

She closed the door as quietly as she could, and looked around her with a deep breath. The curtains had not been opened, so she adjusted them just a chink. Her father wasn't particular - every odd and end in the house was stowed away in here, like the torn rug and the picture of Mount Rushmore. One item she knew she must not touch - the computer. There was the calendar her other grandmother had sent, with her fondest wishes. The calendar seemed to invite her; she poked it from the wall and sat down in the big leather armchair that the dog had peed on. She had an idea.

There was plenty of space inside the cover. Sylvia took a pen from the slipper where she knew her father hid them. She was quite a competent draughtswoman; she drew two recognisable portraits of her brothers. When she had drawn Arthur with wings, and Damien with horns and a tail, she filled the margin with some of the short bad words she had learned from family television.

It still wasn't dinnertime; Sylvia turned the page looking for fresh space. That was when she saw the picture of the swans. They were floating gracefully on a silky green lake, surrounded by naked trees. "If only", she thought, "if only they were real." Suddenly, they began to drift; they were drifting towards her. Sylvia was sitting on a log; she wasn't cold. It was a dry sunny morning, and the sunshine gleamed with a silvery yellow through the misty cloudlets. Outside the study a swirl of hailstones spattered the panes, but the child did not notice.

"I wonder," she thought nervously, "whether they are going to fight me." But they were so beautiful. They skimmed the shimmery water to the shallows and some of them were juvenile swans; they had brown feathers. Sylvia sat as still as a mouse and the four brownish swans plucked themselves out of the water. There were six altogether, and two of them were snowy white - a mother and father, she supposed.

The birds did not seem to mind the child. They were combing their feathers, bending their long necks, rubbing their bills against their plumage; and they were talking to each other. They had golden bracelets around their necks, so Sylvia knew their names. There were two girl-swans called Bubble and Dab. "I'd never know their names," she thought, "if they didn't wear collars."
"What is it?"
"It's a little girl." They had strange voices like wind blowing through bells.
"Can we eat her?"
"Oh no. She wouldn't be good to eat."
"Green-hoppers are very good to eat."
There was a pause while they ruffled themselves and fluffed out their wings so that they looked like a fan.
"I like summer."
"Yes, but today is nice too."
"The yellow light is pretty."
"Yes, but the moonlight is lovely too." The grown up swans did not talk; they just floated quietly in the still water.

Then the four young swans slid into the water, one at a time, gently and silently. They drifted away and when they reached the middle of the pool, they turned their long necks, they flew their wings like pinions, and they looked back at Sylvia. Sylvia looked at them. Their eyes were dark like stones; but they spoke with their movements. Then the stillness broke, because Pip was barking a long way off. The girl woke up to find her head resting on the arm of the leather chair. Her grandparents had arrived.
It was time to find an alibi. So the child stole into the kitchen like a puff of smoke and set to work squeezing lemons. Her father came in with a bottle in one hand, and began to fidget about.

"I can't find the corkscrew, Lilly."
"The sherry is open."
"Hells bells!"
"Use your pen knife, daddy."
"Good thinking!"

Sylvia heard her father opening things in the study, and then there was an angry growl. Oh, rats, he had found the calendar! She was afraid to turn around.

"Well, what have you got to say for yourself?"

Better to be bold. She climbed up on the wooden stool and reached carefully for the powdered sugar, and then descended, and gave a toss.

"Dad, when life gives you lemons, you make lemonade!"

31 December 2002

the pilgrimage

We were delighted when Sr Contritia told us that we were going on a trip to a sacred well. In the west of Ireland it rains for three hundred and sixty-four days. On the other day - it pours. I reminded myself prudently of this and so dressed in layers. I also borrowed an umbrella of Edwardian appearance, with a fearsome leather handle that reminded me of a question mark. As I boarded the bus I felt ready to meet a fate worse than faith.

We passed Rooks Cross, and Sr Contritia said that we were going to say "the fifteen decades of the Rosary". Unfortunately I thought that this was humorous, and I dissolved into giggles. She gave me a quelling look and took out her sturdy prayer beads. I counted on my fingers; of which, luckily, I possessed ten. At the end of the Rosary, we said the litany of Our Lady. "Now," said Sr Contritia, "we shall sing a verse from The Bells of the Angelus."

Time passed, and the mist became driplets. Sr Contritia took out her Rosary beads, and we said the five sorrowful mysteries. Then we recited the litany of Saints, and she told us to sing a verse from The Bells of the Angelus. We disembarked in Ennis, and we all had a bag of chips. Here I tidied myself in the lavatory, where the looking glass was cracked and my reflection had a surreal appearance, like a picture by Dali. The rain was still hesitant, like a sober mourner.

Back on the bus, the landscape was speckled by dolmens. It was like counting sheepherders and I began to doze. When I surfaced again, we were saying the five glorious mysteries, after which we said the litany of Our Lady and sang a verse from The Bells of the Angelus.

At twelve-thirty we left the bus. It was still damp, but not tempestuous. We sat on a low wall, and I had a bag of chips. Then we went to the grotto, where we said the fifteen decades of the Rosary. This time I was able to remain awake, perhaps because the rain had dallied long enough, and there were large and penetrating drops.

We went to pray in a new-art pavilion, which was quite comfortable. My eyes closed. I had the impression someone was saying prayers aloud, into a microphone. He was a tall and magnetic-looking priest, and I was certain that he told us that his name was Father Rhapsody, and that a partner in the hand is worth two in the bush. I awoke to find that a tall and charismatic man was telling us earnestly that it is a very serious matter if you get pregnant - especially for a girl. I also noticed that Sr Contritia was frowning at me. Next there was Confession en masse - as if we were waiting for a lifeboat; we all lined up in a row and told the priest that we were very sorry.

On the way home we said the fifteen decades of the Rosary, and then we all had a bag of chips. Before we alighted Sr Contritia gave us a medallion - a small medal. I pinned mine to my raincoat. In doing so, I collided with my umbrella. The steps were damp. I slipped and found myself standing in the street, as limp as if I was a painting by Salvador Dali - The Persistence of Memory. My friend Amelia approached. Tidy and angelically fair, she might have spent the day in a shoebox instead of in some worthy cause. She very kindly asked me where I had been. I was silent for a moment, and studied her. I had indigestion, my hem was torn, my hair was untidy, and I had a black eye. Yet - best of all - pinned to my lapel was a glorious blue medal.

"Surely," I said, "it must be obvious that I have been on a pilgrimage."
28 October 2002
(Irene Caswell)

40

confessions of a mushroom eater

Mushies, Mushies, out goes the cry
With each wet October that goes by
Whether it be under sun or through raging storm
We start our search afresh with each passing morn
We begin in the mountains and finish in the fields
In our hearts the hope for ever higher yields
The seasoned picker knows all is lost
When appears the season's first frost
So each shortening day is well spent
Scouring grazed fields on one's knees bent
Then my eye spots a fecund brown patch
Of your golden and glistening liberty caps
My soul fills with joy and breathing gets fast
In anticipation of the night's coming bash
Psilocybe semilanceata is the latin name
But its what you do that brought you such fame
Hallucinations, laughter, and bubbling bliss
Are just some of your blessed gifts
As magic mushrooms, you are more commonly known
Magic, even though in piles of shite you make your home
Although your origins stem from lowly dung
Through the ages your praises are loudly sung
By hallucinagenic trippy bards like me
Hippies, school kids, and even professors of mycology
Yea even though you rise from fields of cow flop
I can't think of any other autumnal crop
That I'd rather eat of Halloween night
So to be away with the faeries in flight
So if with these humble words you agree
Come sit down by the fire for a cuppa mushie tea.
(Chris)

night nurse

The year was dying lounged in December.
I was mind locked in its sparse garret.
You whispered softly was I cold
I said "Oh, Yes!"
You wrapped me in a woollen blue blanket.

When unpredictable sleep would not come
You offered me a glass of silky warm milk.
Before I could turn a hesitant "yes" into " no"
You were swiftly gone and smiling you came
 Holding the white glass as high as your name.

An eternity later erratic sleep slid slyly in
Through cascading drips and castle dreams
You were a Queen in a great confused world
Where at your feet robed men laid scalpels and schemes
And blankets and white sheets were unfurled.

terror

The wolf on the hilltop skulking
Watches the sheep graze.
Ah! His eyes are cruel and cunning
Anticipating and then they blaze.
Stealthily he sneaks close
Bared are his salivating fangs
 Then bloody red and buried deep
Into shocked suckling lambs
And terrorised sheep.

Vultures on the treetop swaying
Are watching and waiting.
Crimson and beady eye pulsating
Hearing the falling lambs bleating
They leave the branches circling
Above the panic stricken flock.
Free to stalk the field of death
They descend bickering to the end.
Noisily they gobble hen and cock.

Ah! The nature of bird and animal
So they live and so die.
And we wonder at it and may sigh.
Change to a different scene again
 Think of Herod's murderous men
Or the terrorist in darkly wood
Sometimes a singer of brotherhood
Creeps to kill with crackling gun
His deadly job done away will run.

what if it is true?

What if it is true that he came
Can it be that he was really here?
Immersed in all that squalor and shame
Walking with the crippled and queer?

What if it is true that all that happened
Which has been written repeated and said.
That he was here and seriously grappled
With the problems of quick and dead?

What if it is true they nailed him craven
Under the gloom of a sickly evening sky
Why did he imagine he had been forsaken
When he knew he was destined to die?

Mocked atop that barren and blasted hill
From his eyes beamed no lightening rod
From out his lips a cry his heart to still
But what if it is true that he was God?

the cat

It was a fine June morning after rain.
She crossed the lawn again and again
As if merely touching silkily the grass.
Inside I moved from the windowpane
And watched her go elegantly so.

I have not even a vestige of knowing
Why this morning the sight of her felinity
Fastidiously parading over the wet grass
Cascaded far memories nostalgically down
As into the copse I saw her pass.

As she moved within the green leafy growth
Her eyes were diamonds dancing both
Drawn to steely steady severe focus then
Showing plainly her will was never bent
In any allegiance to the world of men.

Behind the spreading laurel and verdure
I glimpsed her momentarily, a blur of ginger
As taking her tense watchful still stance
She beamed her wildness in a rapacious glance
Evoking an ancient world of terror and romance.

sometimes you haunt me

Sometimes you come to haunt me.
Why did you come to me?
To talk to me and tell
What ill-fated diagnosis had befell
You in the heat of a summer's day.

Drowsy afternoon of summer time
The world was as sweet as wine
With the sent of perfume
Impelling young girls to dance
And dream of love and romance.

You entered steadily in your grey suit
And neat brown tweedy cap
A smile on your pale face
Said the sky had fallen on you
Irrevocably you were ending the race.

Then or never did I know you or of you
Or if your resolve came to pass.
You pledged it surely would.
I believe you meant to make good
Your firm intention to see it through.

Then you slowly solemnly walked away.
I think of the hour of that day.
What I did not say or do
Or what I did not do or say,
Sometimes you haunt me in shades of grey.

may garden

The apple blossoms are falling
Like tears
Carried by the merest hint of
May breeze
In the stillness of mid morning
Adorning into a summer's day.

The mountain ash modestly holds

Its white clusters stately
Swaying so gently it's green livery
To show it is at home
In glory.

The eucalyptus in drooping posture
Tall and adrift like a south sea
Craft
Sailing away from home
Awaiting a stiff wind
To set it's imaging
On grassy foam.
The Japanese maple drenched
In russet red kimono
Moves almost imperceptibly
Subtly changing colours in
It's inner dress to an enchanting
Deepness.

The two young oaks late in
Leafing
Are now up -staging up to impress
Signalling to be a prince and princess.

The stillness of the day
In the garden
With whitethorn and holly
Bordering
Could not be more captivating
For Adam walking those
First days.

He did not know then
There was an ending
To his joy.
And the beauty of sadness
And the sadness of beauty
Is that the falling apple blossom
Is the salty rolling tear
Caught by the sad protruding lip
When we cry.
(John Dillon)

men

Crying into their beers,
Moving up in the world,
Postulating, theorizing,
Picking their noses,

Cheating on their girlfriends,
Scouring their u-bends,
Men

Outdoing each other,
Eating each other's holes,
Signing and posting forms,
Going to the theatre

Looking under hoods,
Receiving stolen goods,
Men

Buying the latest underpants,
Plotting one another's downfall,
Struggling to get out of bed,
Choosing from menus,
Lying about their ages,
Building structures,
Betraying the revolution,
Listening to the streams of their piss,
Hesitating at traffic lights,
Staying to the left side of escalators,

Setting their watches,
Betting on horses,
Men.
(MD - a man)

we're all travellers

We were trying to make it
A nice place to live in
And were banging and nailing
At what was basket-making
In our new institution of a house
We were trying to turn it
Into something to believe in
By pasting and painting
Some gloss of understanding
Over why and what the hell it's all about
And we finally made it
A safe place to stay in
There working and weaving
At our covers for believing
That this is not the final halting site.

48

the nursing home

The nursing home
An island in a sea of green
Is like the titanic
All luxury
But you know it's for the going down

Down its long corridors, gangways
Down to little bedrooms, cabins
Furnished with the bare essentials
For a journey

The passengers sit silent mostly
Or when moving move slowly
Sometimes humming
A sudden remembered tune
And when meeting
On gangways or in Lounges
Greet each other like people on a cruise
Ships that pass in the night
On a journey to no mans land

At the sound of the angelus
They chant
Pray for us now and at the hour
Of our death
No fear no fuss
In spite of knowing 'that each will occupy that final room
The cabin reserved
For those about to disembark

With bars for clinging to
As they nightmare through their plight
And dreams of going down
Through swirling seas of eiderdown
Until they drown
Or wake
To ask what happened
And be told that no one knows

To wait some more, for news,
For relatives from the town
Bringing emergency rations
And talking of rescue
And the two mile journey from the hill
That's now a thousand miles away
And weather and paying the bill
And so on until
They're suddenly gone
Leaving some until a next time
Others forever.

I don't want to go to the home

Please wait until I'm dribbling
It will be just right by then
For it usually comes with incontinence
The same as way back when

You dribbling and incontinent
Were babied in by me
Which hopefully means that in consequence
I can stay till I'm ninety- three

barber's account of Treblinka

The walls were white
Two metres tall
The wire was black
Its holes were small

Outside of this
Was green and fresh
Men fixed a car
Girls stitched a dress
Till their names went on the wall

At nights, farm lights
Seemed not to care
Nor hear the sounds
Of pure despair

As the trains
Came rushing
Stood hissing
Went crashing
Till all that was left, was hair.

new technology

When we were forced to run
John walked
Walked like he'd always done

He didn't aim to win
And those that did
Ran to their death
As if chased by him

Those that fell behind
Died from trying to catch him up

And because of this
And a wide river we came upon
He won.

By walking
Walking like he'd always done,
On water
Us not knowing then
About stilts.

a close shave

If the maid enters with white morning light
And strips away your sheets
Hits straight your bundled pillows
Tips your bed
If she roots amongst old rosaries
Loose wedding rings and fleas
Sorts your live bits from your dead
Drags up your head, from down between
Your knees
If she leaves and you wait
With clenched fist and screaming eyes
Till you reason to rise
Wash cook and go
And if while doing so
Realise its not your room
Ring reception
And book another life.

just a thought

Watching my happy husband eat
What I was happy to cook
Had me think that perhaps my life is just a tasty snack.

That perhaps I am sacrificial lamb
That's eaten at leisure by some happy god
Or maybe gobbled by a gob

And that whether I'd come
As door mouse or king
I am to be devoured by the thing
That makes breaks and eats me

Continuously
Like forever and ever
Amen.

bar thoughts in England

Come soon the day I sail away
To my own Innisfree
And there to think with tea to drink
And a fag to comfort me

Come soon the time I leave the grime
Of London's hard E3
Where my way out is with black stout
And pints of Tenants E

Come Innisfree when my new me
Will eat sweet cake at three
And there set seed without the weed
And maybe grown sweet pea

Come soon black crows and purple sloes
And a head that's Guinness free
Where mild police maintain the peace
And sky, is not TV
(P.J. Fitzgerald)

hope for darkness - for victims of despair September 1995

You rise before the waking sun
yet lose the race before its run,
and sink into the pools of blood,
the swelling blackness is in flood.

You skip in hope along the shore
knowing life could hold much more,
but you were born into a snare
that seems to choke the more you dare.

But like the single, simple ray of light
that cuts the vast and empty void
Your spark too can again explode to life
And melt the jagged steel of despair
        Believe it!

to a girl on the verge
On the train from Porto Ercole to Rome 9-8-1998

Beauty sulking sleekly in your heart
turning thoughts that kindle fiery eyes
love knows not, nor mind can know ALL truth
   yet on, around
   in, along and through life's spinning circles
   all your words and silences are beautiful and warm and pure.

Fly from here and
paddle the streams torrential
carried along, forging ahead,
controlling, sinking, falling,
arising again from the rocks of insecurity;
At last to calmly flow
into the wide wholesome sea of womanhood;
flowering forth out of why and how
into You, serene and beautiful
that I so love and adore.

a piece of fiction, all the much October 1998
A belt of reality for which I am deeply grateful

What happened on Sunday evening at 6.30?
If something real happened?.........if(?)
how can I go on living this charade?

What seemed to have happened was that E**** and I were walking down
the road to Rathmines. We/I were talking agitatedly about the WHY of
EVERYTHING.......in a flippant way, yes, I admit .... whylifewhylightwhy-
dark whyalifeprocess WHYWHYWHYWHYWHYWHYWHYWHYWHYWHY-
WHYWHY WHYWHYWHYWHYWHYWHYWHYWHYWHYWHYWHYWHYWHY-
WHYWHYWHYWHYWHYWHYWHYWHYWHYWHYWHY.....when....."I"...stop
ped ....ques...tion....ing ..... and .... realising/realised...... slowly that
everything everything thing things around around around US US US me
you him US .. was strangely :..... suddenly..... muted .... transformed
  I felt I was dreaming

I felt surrounded by imaginary ghostly things
I felt as if my mind glowed and was raised infinitely up
I felt my normal self as but a speck at the bottom of that consciousness
YET I myself felt TINY before a hugeness which seemed to be immersing me
with itself
it was all happening
    Time stopped. MY WORLD STOPPED
tears flowed down my eyes tears of regret and fear that it was all over
(I thought for a moment it was, it seemed as though I was being pulled up
away out of this world -and it could have been did I wish to go)
THEN tears of joy that life,that the life I shared in, was really SO HUGE AND
SO WONDERFUL.
Joy at my "discovery".........and fear...great fear
Yet I did not want to leave, and leave myself as I am in this world
1) I felt I was not ready
2) I felt I could do "good" HERE to aid others to realise the "true" nature
of their self.
SO I clung to my friend who was going through something similar, and said
no, no I don't want to go.............

but now my sense of purpose has been totally put out and I find it hard to
focus on the normaleveryday life as it proceeds around its like as if I knew
too much and that that, HERE, is too little, or does not help me at all.
Can I refind World Perspective and a sense of life-time to be able to live and
grow and operate here?
(These words describe at best a minimal part of what actually happened)

earth, world, universe, all.
Tuesday, 7-11-2000 @ ted's in Limerick.

Earth, World, Universe, All.
Forgive us for being so small;
I rise up out of myself and these other selves to gaze upon us.
Forgive us. Here we are breathing in this smoke, pouring this poison into
us.
Forgive us.
Outside the universe smiles and shines.
In here, we are cold and dark in our warmth.
We are lonely and free in the heat of the night.
Forgive us for seeing so little.
Forgive us for nailing our minds into this box.

Trees shudder in the evening air.
Crows caw and cut black shadows across a yellow moon.
The rivers run and run,
flowing ever on to seadom.

Cosmic Currents!
Seep into us!
Raise us up.
Make us one with you.
Make us feel a part of what you are,
Seeing out of this, our self-made shell.

travelling on a train in france February 4 2000

Once again I come to thinking about the emptiness of the individualist life structure which is held up as a model for people.

I get on the train.

I walk through the carriages to find my seat. Car number 20, seat 47. Right at the back of the train. Walking between the rows of seats, I feel people's eyes on me. In silence, people sitting comfortably in their allotted places; comfortable or uncomfortable from their identities, they look out at me, their penetrating eyes seeming to shout:

"Who are you?"

They judge me, seeming to say to themselves:

"Is he better than me?"

"Oh look at him! Well, I'm certainly more good-looking than he is."

The eyes, the eyes. These eyes which put a silent insurmountable wall between us. Me too. Feeling the eyes, I stand up straighter, trying to project someone who is as strong, independent, and self-confident as possible.

How absurd that is! All these people trying desperately to be Someone, on their own.

All these people trying to be self-contained, solitary units, with no need of anyone else.

Of course people should develop their minds and bodies as much as possible. The only way to do this is by having the liberty to live and work as one wishes. That is the Humanist idea. Self-development.

However, the goal is not to be able to FINALLY ignore other people, to at last be totally independent of them.

How absurd that is. Earth, our home, so small, here and now, floating, somewhere, in the immensity of time and space. We are so many, each of us is such a small part of the whole. We look so alike. SURELY, the End of Self-development is not to learn how to live in isolation, but how best to function as a human being. How best to function as a member of the human race.

Working for ourselves! And then, not even for ourselves, but for our cars, houses, household appliances, working for our wallet. Things, merely things, with nothing at all to do with us as people

Working for things. A work as useless in life as it is in death. Death, remember that?

a selection of reality sandwiches January 2001

My friends.

We are strange creatures all the same. Bits of flesh and bone. Loving, striving, hating, killing, reproducing, building, singing, dying. Alone here, on this pale blue dot we call Earth, our home, which spins around a fireball sun that will itself, one day, like all things, cease to be.

As Carl Sagan said: "Humans are a rare as well as endangered species. Every one of us is, in the cosmic perspective, precious. If a human disagrees with you, let him live. In a hundred billion galaxies, you will not find another."

That's what is needed, the cosmic perspective, on ourselves, on others, on the world. Not the jaded "been there done that" approach that kills off our natural, necessary curiosity. Life is mystery. We don't know what it's about! We are strange creatures. Strange mixtures of emotional and rational quantities. We think of ourselves as the dominant species. We are. But we are still a species. We were produced by Mother Earth. We are part of her. And so must live in harmony with her ways. Or else die as a race. It's a choice.

Only that our mindsets are still too much conditioned by Judaeo-Christian thinking: "Increase and multiply, fill the earth and conquer it." That perhaps served a purpose once. As did religious laws and rules. Not God, not Allah, not Shiva can give us the perspective we now need, as a species, to decide where we're going. Organised Religion has probably done more harm than good, with its rules and regulations. DO THIS. DON'T DO THAT. Why? BECAUSE GOD SAYS SO. And so we didn't think for ourselves, about our choices, just blindly obeyed the laws dictated by the Church.

But we don't need God to know what is good, bad, right, wrong. The German philosopher showed that in his book Beyond Good and Evil. He railed against the Church as propagators of a sickly, ANTI-LIFE, morality. He was one of the first UNIVERSALISTS. He saw that the laws of nature are what count, not human interpretations of what an unseen divine presence requires from us. That's what we need today. The cosmic perpective.

The cosmic perspective. We are so taken up with the intricacies of the Human system in which we live, that we ignore the ways of the Life system. Consequently, we are not aware of the damage that we do to it, and ultimately to ourselves.

Human society is not reality.

Cars, toasters, Tv, houses, the greed to be rich, hatred, wars, suicide, perversion.

This is not reality. This is Human reality. The world that we have built is the product of our imagination, not Natures, even though people continue to misuse Darwin's "survival of the fittest" theory in order to justify DOG-EAT-DOG capitalism as the most natural system. It is not. Nature does not self-destruct. Man has a mind. The most natural thing for him would be to use it, to meet the needs of people today without affecting the ability of future peoples to meet theirs. A sustainable development. Not the present Unnatural system. According to Atomic Physicist Victor Wiesskopff, the only thing in nature which ressembles the present model of Economic development is..............cancer.

So, my disease-ridden brothers and sisters, let not all our studies, our hobbies, our talk, and our jobs be contributions to the sickness. Let's be part of the cure. First we cure ourselves, by undoing the conditioning we have endured from this sick society which promotes a fake way of being "radically estranged from the structure of our being" (R.D. Laing), then, we cure eachother, and our world. The revolution will not be televised, sang Gil-Scott Heron. No. It will be the inevitable revolution of which Tolstoy wrote on his deathbed. The revolution of men's hearts. The revolution of awareness, as we alter the structure of our minds and our being.

"All matter is merely energy condensed to a slow vibration, we are all one consciousness, experiencing itself subjectively, we are the imagination of ourselves, there is no such thing as death and life is only a dream." Bill Hicks

Changing ourselves, we change the world. We have a choice. Lets start.

........but then it's easier to follow, isn't it. And everyone else really do seem to know what they're doing........I think......

We've been a disease for so long up now that it feels kind of comfortable.

fragmentation of the self March 2001

The binding glue of childhood's bloom is gone,
the remnants of things great
the remnants of that bit of light left in the darkness
remnants of ideas
will to be
remnants of honesty
remnants of sincerity
remnants of times back then when things seemed to have a meaning
remnants of times when it seemed that meaning could really be found
        not just made or invented

Society, Changes, Evolution, Entropy, Degeneration.
I'm not sure all these people know what they're doing......
Male, female, working, mating, loving, killing.......
Killing for the unbearable lack of structure or sense.....
Victims of too much inquiry and too few answers

I've just seen a group of kids bullying a red-haired boy at a bus-stop...
I've just seen myself in one of their faces, a loud, awkward, chubby youth
on a scooter.....as I was back then....house angel, street devil....picking
only on the weaker ones, and making sure they were never too big.

I think I live in an in-between period where Man is at a critical phase, and
must decide between evolution and decay. I find myself, like many others,
in this period of indecision and confusion.
I re-read those words "indecision and confusion". Exactly my state.....inde-
cision and confusion....so....afterall, maybe man's fate lies with me and
what I decide.
Will I be a part of Evolution or Decay?
("I": identification of the self as separate from the world.)

prayers
Thursday 03-05-2001. Dolan's Warehouse, Limerick.

1)
If only I could be free.
If only my self could unself itself and I could see.
If only I could know the right way to be and escape from these manacles of "me".
Something real to unlock and share and live.

2)
I am in a night club now
I am surrounded by voices, glinting glasses, clothes, bodies, and lights, yet my mind is with the crow, the poorest, most ragged, unseen, unthought of and forgotten crow.
Claws clinging to a branch in moonlight cold, alone beneath the stare of solitary stars.
A being in the world, with us and without us, my mind is with you, crow, and I am alone here among these people.

the fall of america

Silence.
I turn off the radio. Again.
I can't sleep.

Mind-voice of Irishman in the quiet of a 3.39am Dublin night: I heard the voices of the young Americans; I televisionally saw their structures brought down in smoke and flames, the people jumping from windows, the city coughing in a cloud of poisonous dust.

The single greatest Terrorist attack in American History.

My heart goes out to all the hurt. To all the hurt and friends of hurt. To all the dead and friends of dead. To all the burnt, bent and broken.
To all the innocent.
To all the innocent.
To all the innocent.

As innocent as the villages wiped out in Guatemala by a dictatorship created and armed by the Military-Industrial complex elite government of the United States of America. For What? To protect the United Fruit Company, many of whose directors were key members of the US establishment, whose profits were being threatened by the land reform and redistribution desired by the Guatemalan people. They too were innocent. But the American elite likes 'free trade'.

Innocent like the people of Indonesia, Vietnam, Cambodia, Laos, East Timor, Chile, El Salvador, Nicaragua, Kurdistan, Iraq....pawns in a game of global economic power play, victims of America's attempts to protect its interests, the interests of 'world trade'.
No. Not victims of America. Victims of the power hungry elite that controls and leeches America through the Democrat/Republican charade.

The shit hits the fan at last.
The U.S. people get a horrific dose of what its own government has been freely dealing in for the last 50 years:
        Sheer Bloody Terror.
Welcome to the world that you have helped create.

To all the hurt and friends of hurt. To all the dead and friends of dead. To all the burnt, bent and broken.
To all the innocent.
To all the innocent.
To all the innocent.
ALL ALL ALL ALL

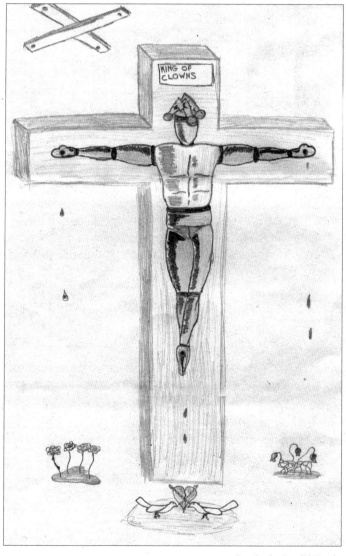

Drawing by Gearóid Murphy

Charleville(i) December 2001

Lots of spaces.....
Lots of places.....
Lots of people....
With lots of thoughts....
Lots of actions....
Lots of inactions....
Lots of cruelty...
Lots of love....
Lots of sadnesses...
Some laughter and happiness....
Lots of alcohol...
Lots of nicotine and tobacco...
Lots of desire laughter anger spite hate love bewilderment confusion that breaks out with the overflow of alcohol...
Lots of some people just not into all that who lead quietly brilliant, evil or nonedescript country lives away from Mr and Mrs Publicly Gas Man and Woman with often dismally sad private lives......
Lots of people who allow their truer selves be compromised by the desire to fit in with the rest.....even though 'the rest' are also themselves just trying to fit in with the rest....in fact everyone is trying to conform to a 'norm' that exists only in people's perceptions......in fact there is no norm.....its all wide open.....

The 'norm' is a long history of people trying to conform to an imaginary 'norm'....
The 'norm' is the repression of the imagination.

Imagination. Freedom.
Freedom of the self.
No need to construct a Public Face to cover over the inner tumults that every body is afraid to show...
What about bringing about a situation where the lack of a Public Face is taken as a sign of courage/honesty/holiness?

There is political freedom......
But there is also mental freedom....
And both have to be won with long and joyous battle....
Don't doubt it......

(no title) January 2003-02-17

-     Oh Christ! Not another rain pome!
-     Yes Christ, another rain word-flow-out-of-soul, for this whole town is being washed by a January drizzle.

Feet splash, cars sizzle on the streets and water streams down the spattered dripping window panes.
The town cries, my thinking mind begins to sink on the flood of its sorrows and my swelling heart sets sail on a life-raft of emotion.
I stand around looking lost and bewildered; people may look and wonder 'what is that fella at, with that glazed look on his face?', 'is he on drugs?'....ah but I don't even give a fuck enough not to give a fuck.
It doesn't matter.
I'm not on drugs.
I'm on life.
I am alive.

Standing there dreaming dreams
dreams less and less rooted in all that I think I know,
dreams that I know would lead to where not many people go,
dreams that call me on to exile, solitude and adventure.

The rain rains on,
I am warmed by the glowing chill of my melancholy.

-     Don't dream too far, dear heart, many are those who dreamed too far in this town and died or were killed in the prevaling cold and misunderstanding.
-     No, I won't dream too far;
I'll let my heart sob and cry,
And take this time to float in the tears of the world
But they will never submerge me,
For I will rise,
In my own way,
When the time is right,
As the chains of conformity dissolve
    And we grow to live holy lives of beautiful freedom and goodness.

heal January 2003
Lines written on a piece of tissue paper in 3am Cork city coffee-house.

Heal, Heal, Heal, Heal
Heal my brains
Heal my eyes
Heal ears
Heal my lips
Heal my tongue
Heal my languages
Heal my fingers
Heal my feet, my toes, ankles, legs, knees, thighs, testicles, cock.
Heal my stomach
Heal my chest
Heal my skin
Heal the hairs which grow out of my head

Heal my thoughts
Heal my words
Heal the waves and rivers of my emotions

Heal my hate
Heal my spite
Heal my ugliness
Heal my selfishness
Heal the hurt I have left with others
Heal my murdering
Heal my murderers
Heal the killers, the killed and the killing
Heal the bombs they drop that scald and burn and sear,
Heal the whole flood of endless tears

Heal the lost,
Heal our unknowing
Heal our unloving
Heal our uncaring
Heal my uncaring
Heal my unawareness, cruelty and disregard.

Heal the solitude, the fear and the lonesomeness

Heal my sadness and make me laugh with the morning bird-song

Heal us humans
Heal us humans
Heal us humans
Heal, Heal, Heal, Heal.......
Suuntee, suuntee, suuntee....suantrí, suantrí

Let me know real love not lust
Let me care deeply for every last leaf which is blown on the world's winds.

Let me see and feel the hurts and joys in all things.

Let me cry when I cry
Let me laugh when I laugh
Let me breathe when I breathe
Let me sing when I sing
Let us grow when we grow
Let us build, believe and love
Really building, really believing, really loving
Always until the dying end screeching out
great gasps of soulful desperate thankfulness for the miracle flash of elec-
tric being which we were allowed to live.
("gerald" "fitzGibbon")

wind dance

Today, I felt the wind.
It blew right through me.
I saw a young girl standing on the edge of a cliff.
She cried aloud.
Her voice was carried on the wind.
I heard her pain.

I closed my eyes
and breathed in the smell
of her disappointment.
Arms outstretched:
I felt her move.

She danced on the wind
and came home
to shelter in the fortress of my breast.

infidel

I close my eyes.
  A dog barks.
  A bird chirps.
Wind dances
through leaves that rustle in response.

I could be anywhere;
a rock in Connemara,
or a Kerry beach
but I am far from home
in desert land.

Sun shines.
Dust blows hot against my skin.

I am safe here,
behind high walls
which hide my pale skin.

Prayer chant breaks the silence
and think of the craziness
out there,
outside,
beyond my cocoon.

I am an infidel in a foreign land.
(Fiona Buckley-Fitzpatrick)

from my hospital bed

It's the 3rd of December 2000 as I lie in my hospital bed with tubes hanging out of me from all angles. I feel very weak and not for the first time in the past twenty-four hours my bedclothes are sodden with cold sweat and need to be changed once more. One eye is focused on the tube, which is draining fluid from my stomach. It's very uncomfortable and hard to swallow my spittle as the tube through my nose to the stomach is blocking the passage and I have an awful choking sensation. A saline drip is helping me from becoming too dehydrated. In short I am nailed to the bed and most likely will be in this situation for some days to come more if the drainage continues. I am wondering where all the gunge is coming from and constantly checking the weight of the bag, which is suspended from a bracket on the side of the bed. I can tell by the weight at this stage when the bag is full which indicates that tomorrow is going to be another day of misery. I can't sleep and every hour is like an eternity.

My other eye is fastened on the television on the other side of my room and I must try to concentrate on the film, which has just started. At least my favourite actor Jack Nicholson is playing the lead and the film is poignantly called, "As Good As It Gets". Neither is anything going right for Jack; the waitress who serves him at this favourite restaurant is leaving which is causing him much trauma. He cannot bear the thought of any other serving him and will take whatever steps are necessary to persuade her to keep her job. 'This guy is a complete nutter', she tells a friend. She's right of course. Things that would be trivial to others are astronomical to Jack and of course in my situation I can identify with him totally. The dog that he reluctantly took-in from a neighbour is now giving him solace and at this stage they have grown to love one another. Now the wanker of a neighbour - whom both Jack and myself took exception to from the beginning - is knocking on the apartment door and shouting that he wants his dog back. I couldn't stop myself from shouting 'You rotten bastard' at the television. Can anything be worse? I ask myself.

The bed is absolutely sodden now and I am telling myself it cannot be totally blamed on my present condition. There has to be an element of cold turkey causing my misery and for the exercise and to keep my mind busy I go back over the past thirty years (as an easy figure to work on without a calculator) and I come up with a figure of 90,000 units of alcohol has passed through my system in that time. This is not the true figure; I should add another seventeen years intake to find the correct figure.

"Fuck it", I say to myself, that figure can't be right. Forget it and try to concentrate on the film.

The saga began a week ago. I had an arrangement made with my rheumatologist to present myself at the reception of the Orthopaedic hospital for further tests to try to resolve a persistent problem in my right foot, which continued to "pinch" while walking. Already blood tests and x-rays showed nothing abnormal. However a CAT scan would most likely show up what was causing the discomfort, followed by the necessary steps to hopefully be able to play golf and walk my dogs, pain free. I had taken my car to the hospital and would be home in 2/3 days at most.

But the night before I awoke with a bad pain in my stomach, which I thought would pass, it didn't. However I thought one thing at the time and the leg was for now a priority. Three days later I drove myself to another hospital and had the CAT scan. My plan was that when driving myself back to the Orthopaedic hospital I would call to a chemist and get something for the stomach. I found I had left my money on my bedside locker and so that plan was jeopardized. Back in my bed the pain got worse and when I couldn't take any more I called the Nurse who in turn phoned the doctor. I was subsequently whisked by ambulance to the South Infirmary where a doctor who for means of identification I will call V.J. and two nurses were waiting. The immediate x-ray showed I had a blockage in the intestine.

I overheard one nurse say to the other: "Fair play to him,"(V.J.) "he spotted it straight away."

While one nurse held me, the other inserted a tube through my nose into my stomach, which was a terrible experience but began to drain off fluid immediately.

Four days later and still on a drip, the surgeon said I would have one more x-ray and if he was satisfied, the tube could come out and I would be on sips of water for a further twenty four hours and hopefully progress to slowly introduce small amounts of solid food. Passing wind proved to be a very important factor with my complaint because every time a nurse or doctor entered my room, it was the first question asked. "Yes" I lied most of the time. However, as luck would have it, this morning when the nurse asked the question, I had the urge to break wind and without further ado I released a most horrendous fart, the likes of which was never recorded in that hospital. She left the room happy and smiling saying: "Good man yourself". I nearly laughed myself sick at the outrage. It was the first laugh I got in the past week; the blockage was clear, I hoped. The final x-ray would be clear, I prayed, and all the tubes hanging from me would be gone. My claustrophobia had taken a bad hammering.

When taking off my dressing gown after the x-ray I dislodged the needle feeding the drip into my vein and a doctor had to be found to put this matter right once more. An eternity passed before a young doctor emerged and, despite several attempts, he failed to find a vein. My veins had collapsed, he said and left to find a more experienced doctor. I was by now very dehydrated and shaking when V.J. arrived and eventually found the desired vein and quickly put me up on a drip which he said had to get into me quickly. As I watched the drip,drip,drip into my vein I became light headed which I sensed was par for the course. V.J. had been very smart in not telling me he was about to take out the tube and he did it so quickly that I hardly noticed. When 3 litres of saline liquid had entered my system, the drip was taken away and hourly sips of water was the order for that day.

The daily routine involved blood tests, injections into my belly to prevent blood clots. Throughout my stay I had to wear a pair of white elastic tights, - which I displayed to visitors and asked them to organise Ballet lessons for me - again to stop blood clots in my legs.

There are handy and awkward people in every walk of life and I met one of the latter. A frog-faced nurse who kept looking at herself in the mirror while poking for a vein. The butchery was most likely caused by what she saw in the mirror. Getting to the jax at the other end of the room was achieved with the help of one of Pat Burke's "Stingingators". (One might ask what is a "stingingator". The answer is there is no such thing or word. It was conceived by a Carpenter when he came across a group of people on Charleville's Main Street who were gaping into the engine of a Baby Ford Motor Car and giving their varied opinions as to why the car wouldn't start. At that time when there were far more horses and carts on the streets, people stopped to look in wonder at Henry Forde's horseless carriage. The carpenter who knew everything peered over the groups' shoulders and announced that the "stingingator" - a vital ingredient of the internal combustion engine - was gone and so a new word entered the English language in 1948.) Imagine a loaded bag in one hand, terrified it would fall and pull the tube from my stomach, while the other hand had to guide the gantry holding the drip as I hobbled along at a snails pace on one leg to my destination. When I eventually got there in a state of exhaustion, to direct the weaponry toward the WC to urinate, which at the time infuriated me, was nothing short of a work of art. Not many people know that those saline drips are much more potent than porter for frequency.

I suppose it was because of the fact that I was being questioned ten times a day if I had passed wind that the phenomenon began to manifest itself on a scale which heretofore never entered my mind. For instance I couldn't imagine the Queen ever breaking wind; for some reason I could imagine a flatulent Queen Mother. I put that down to her supposed liking for Gin. Terry Keane never, certainly not in Charlie's company. To save embarrassment in certain circumstances we have all had to tighten up to suppress a fart, which is categorized as the height of ignorance in company and always denied by the culprit. Whereas in hospital the unfortunates with similar intestinal problems, the act is almost a cause for celebration and congratulations and backslapping and a cause for concern and shame to those who's answer to the question is "No". For comparative reasons, can you imagine walking down the street and instead of the usual "good morning" salutation, you asked everyone on route if they passed wind. Instead of back slapping as in hospital, there would be fistfights at every street corner throughout the world and brawls all over the place. One would be castigated as pig-ignorant and possibly jailed as being the instigator of the rumpus. It's a very strange phenomenon indeed and we have the arrogance to blame the cows farting for damage to the ozone layer.

While in the twilight zone I had the most amazing dreams, two of which are vivid in my mind.
Two pigeons used to spend the night on a ledge outside my window. They would herald their arrival with a few Coos. It was the night I tried to concentrate on the film "As Good As It Gets" and when I eventually passed out, I dreamt I sprouted wings and together with my two pigeons flew into the sky doing fast fancy turns reminiscent of the "Red Arrows". The one thing that confused me or seemed unnatural was the fact that the two pigeons had Jack Nicholson heads on them that constantly kept smiling at me.
The second vivid dream involved two of my friends J.O'R and DB. It was Kilkee in 1958 as I entered the Strand Hotel. The clanging of ware in the dining room signified they were laying up for lunch and John, the waiter smiled at me as I passed. He looked as young as ever. I proceeded to the back lounge and low and behold there was DB standing in the middle of the lounge surrounded by a bevy of beautiful girls and commanding centre stage as usual. I asked: "What in the hell are you doing here?" and he replied that he had just been appointed MC by Mrs. McMahon for the season - fed and found. I couldn't believe it and in a fit of temper and jealousy stormed out of the hotel to my car, ZB 9937. I felt JO'R should get

this bad news immediately and I drove in haste to Kilmallock. I even passed Fanny O'Deas without stopping which illustrated the urgency of my mission. JO'R was standing at the door of his butcher stall, his coat covered in blood and about to close for the night as I broke the news.

"I'm on my way back from Kilkee," I told him "and you'll never guess who's after getting the appointment of MC for the season at the Strand Hotel." He was equally enraged when I told him. Sure he said he is only 18 years of age and is hardly known in Kilkee. "'Tis a terror," he said "that one of us were not considered after all the times we did MC for Mrs. McMahon and never got as much as a thank you or a pint from the establishment. I bet Joe Gibson didn't approve the appointment.".

Eventually the penny dropped. It had to take Pull to get this important job, we agreed, and most likely an approach to the Hotel Manager was made on his behalf, probably by Garret Fitzgerald. And then I woke up.

(Dave Foley, December 2000.)

autumn

Golden rays of sun break in, through rain stained bars it's spring again,
But stop, it's I the fool to kid myself. The sun shone once just to please
itself,
And looking out across my view life is dying and so I too
Must stand apart if need arise and go saying gently to myself
Its late this year is spring.
(Jamesie Foley)

insignificant whispers

Never was one to sing the blues
though at times I wish I would.
Instead I narrate the tale of my so-called life
and regale the new generation with out of context
sparsely exaggerated renditions of previous events

Content to lend an ear albeit for the grace and
goodwill, though more precautious and
timid on new territory, aided by the numbers which
I feel we lacked. Able to hold on to and
perhaps realise some day their dream(s).

Heart wrenching riffs, heart breaking lyrics
inside the white rabbit's head there are many
things afoot between the stars and the fallen
idols; resentment for the fallen stars and false
icons especially red 7 he calls for "RED RUM"

This skeletal support system can only really
be broken from the pink side out not the
right side skin. Who are we but the
masters or apprentices of our support system.
Tragic suicide but not so much so as we
maybe will never reach our full capacity

The voltage will remain steady until it
is broken. Explore, expand and empathise
light the clown's nose, be the freak without
need of a leash. Experience exercise experiment
with the collective temperament of within.

song

Wired to the moon, I can't fall asleep
Shut me down, over-worked and at my peak,
I can't stand this deprivation of mine
Body shut down, brain's awake but I'm dyin

Up again, go again, no damn time
Up again, go again, I'm hostage in my life

Don't mean it when I do,
don't say it when I should

but you know me better
than I ever could

up again, go again, no damn mind
up again, go again, no freedom as a right

I just called to say I'm tired
too much caffeine once again wired
keeps me on my toes
tells me when to go

(no title)

Behind closed doors her life is forsaken.
True mind's word/s from her eyes there for the taking.
Stop where you are
Throw out the conflict
Live alone and hide
No one will ever love you
In this world so wrongly abused.

He is the victim of his own unreasonable self-hatred,
Lays his hands upon her shoulder and his fist to her head
Numb as he now looks up
Only to see and wish to feel the darkness of this rectangular case.
No rhyme or reason
No lullabies
Just the discord of his deserved murder.

thought

Thought influences my actions but why not the antithesis? I ponder. As the
sun gives way to the night, so does night return to day and life.
There is no rhyme or reason to thought, it mainly exists as we do, in all its
unequivocal glory and solemn fidelity, it is constant. As the soul searches,
the mind remains untouched. Physically it is intangible, emotionally
rendering itself vulnerable, like the last leaf on Autumn's tree, so it will fall,
but not before you do, for you it will clip the melancholy of drama and
evoke sentiments of final fantasy, euphoria and yet regret.
Thought influences us all, I ask why not live in unending harmony.
(D. Herlihy)

alive

Jaded plants
rain sodden greenery
A single snowdrop
radiates energy

Winter muted
dark defeated
Budding white survivors
Spring's heart beat

brightest star

Storm clouds shroud the brightest star
but it shines despite their fury
Pollution dims the dazzling light
Dawn blurs it's brilliance

But high above the silent desert
it gleams and glistens
with shimmering splendour
Ever visible to those
who risk the journey
into darkness.

to a midwinter's daisy

You caught me in full stride
I stopped to pick you
for preservation
between the pages of a book.
But your midwinter face
beamed so brightly.
I could not drain your solstice sap.

I touched your radiant petals
leaving a thumb print
on your seed-full core.

I don't need a daisy bookmark.
You have marked the earth tilt
and are shining in my soul.

white

Milky white the galaxy
that caps our hemisphere.
Urgent white the mountain streams
hungry for the sea.
Icy white the frosty sprites
that play in the frozen grass.
Niagara white the water sprites
that slide down Poll an Eas.
Fresh-air white the lichen blotches
On granite and limestone.
Watery white the river bubbles
Curling into foam.
Fragile white the spider's web
Woven on the stiffened bush.
Silver white the mountain mist
Veiling mid-winter's blush.
Radiant white our inner light
beckoning us to connect
to our awesomeness and beauty
and sit as silent guests.
(Bernadette Maria Knopek)

a very special child

A meeting was held quite far from this earth,
it's time again for another birth.
Said the angels to the Lord above:
"This special child will need much love.

His progress may seem very slow,
accomplishments he may not show.
And he'll require extra care,
from the folks he meets down there.

He may not run or laugh or play,
his thoughts may seem quite far away.
In many ways he won't adapt,
and he'll be known as handicapped.

So lets be careful where he's sent,
we want his life to be content.
Please Lord, find the parents who,
will do a special job for you.

They will not realize right away,
the leading role they're asked to play,
But with this child sent from above,
comes stronger faith and richer love.

And soon they'll know the privilege they're given,
in caring for this gift from heaven.
Their precious charge so meek and mild,
is heavens very special child."

alone at christmas

We post cards to one another at this time of the year,
and wish each other happiness as Christmas day draws near.
We all go to mass that morning, join our hands kneel down and pray,
and think of the little baby who once in a manger lay.

Do we try to do what he done I know he wish we would,

and suffer just a little to do other people good.
Do we think of all the old folk who are living on their own,
since their family has left them they spend Christmas all alone.

As they sit in their little cabin I am sure that we all know,
they think of happy Christmas's in the years long, long ago.
When Santa came on Christmas Eve to their little girls and boys,
and the joy on Christmas morning showing Mam and Dad their toys.

And when the Children grow up and yes, that is the way,
they are settled down and married now in lands far, far away.
And the mother she got feeble one cold winter's day she died,
the old man shed some lonely tears, as he sat there by her side.

Yes now he's poor and lonely, please do understand,
will someone call to see him and give him a helping hand.
Then the letterbox it rattles, he looks over at the door
and sees a Christmas letter lying near it on the floor.

It surprises him when he sees it, from who now could it be,
thank God there may be some one that might have thought of me.
Perhaps from John or Mary, yes that is what I hope,
and he squeezes the letter tightly, then he kisses the envelope.

He cries and reads the letter, just picture it if you can,
it was from one he always loved, his little daughter Ann.
She said "A happy Christmas Dad, 'tis sad poor Mam is gone,
I am sending you some money and I hope twill help you on.

I can't do all the things I want, this very hard you know,
to give happiness like you gave us on Christmas's long ago."
He blessed himself and thanked the Lord, Oh yes he done what's right,
his loving daughter thought of him, he'll sleep in peace tonight.

But remember there are old folk, oh God it isn't fair,
whose Children just ignore them, just forget that they are there.
So if you know those people, will you please give them a call,
and make their Christmas happy and God will bless ye all.

on the tear

Now when I get drunk, my wife she gets mad,
When I stagger in home, she gets sore.
So last Christmas Eve sure I made a vow,
And promised I'd get drunk no more.

Yes all the day long sure I stayed in at home,
My wife said "You're doing what's right."
But I said I'd go look for the Echo,
About ten apast six that night.

I thought my poor head it felt dizzy,
I'd terrible pain in my back.
I said I'd get something to cure it,
So I rambled into Tom Stack.

I said give me a packet of aspirins,
To take all this soreness away,
But Tom said the aspirins are no good,
Drink that drop, 'tis a much better way.

Yes after a few I felt better,
The pain it all left my by japers.
So I shock hands with Tom and I thanked him,
And I said I'll go look for the paper.

When I got far as the Hole in the Wall,
Be gob sure I'm telling no lie.
I opened the door and went in there,
Just to look for the paper boy.

Mick Conner wished me Happy Christmas,
He said are you going on a spree.
I said no thank you I'm taking nothing,
He said you'll have to have something with me.

So after Tom Stack and Mick Conners,
I was feeling quiet happy and frisky.
Believe me that's how 'twould effect you,
After drinking a share of good whiskey.

Now when I came out of O'Connor's,
The rain it poured down from the sky.
So I slipped for a while in to Ryan's
Just to let the shower pass by.

There was a big crowd inside in Dave Ryan's
I'm not going to mention their names.
They were talking of Rugby and Football,
and all kinds of different games.

Tough men full of brains and muscle,
You couldn't get worse if you tried.
And they all looked so quiet and so gently,
With their beautiful wives by their side.

They were all drinking whiskey and porter,
I called for a bottle of beer.
I drank some and then asked the question,
Who'll win the all Ireland next year.

There were shouts then for Cork and Tipperary,
Some fellow said God only know's,
So I said 'twas time to be going,
I might meet Mickey Brien at Leo's

In there 'twas real Christmas,
A lot of my pals were there.
They wished me all the very best,
Drinks came from everywhere.

I said have ye the evening paper,
For the Echo I am trying.
Tom Ward came in saying the paperboy,
Is below in Pat O'Briens.

Pat Ryan wouldn't let me go,
Saying drink this other one.
By the time I staggered into Brien's,
The paperboy was gone.

I was so fed up I took a drink,
Then I came out on the street.
And just near Feeney's corner,
An old friend I did meet.

I staggered half way down Broad Street,
As if I got a push,
I said to my pal Happy Christmas,
Cone on we'll go in the Bush.

When we came out of the Bush bar,
My friend said I'll bet you a crown.
That you are forgetting your paper,
So the two of us crawled up the town.

On yes I was half drunk and fed up,
I always remember it well.
When I said come on we might get one,
Inside McCarthy's Hotel.

I tripped on the step at the door way,
And fell on my flat in the hall.
I cursed and roared out in temper,
When they said they'd no paper at all.

We sat on a lovely soft couch there,
And said we'd take our time.
We started on the small ones,
And the two of us drank whiskey and lime.

When we came out of there we felt groggy,
We had no feeling in our poor feet.
But still we crawled on bit by bit,
To Wilson's down Chapel Street.

I cried have ye the paper,
We want to read the news.
Old Paddy started laughing,
Saying I think ye're on the booze.

Oh I was going to hit him,
And bust his fat old head.
But straight away I changed my mind,
And had a pint instead.

How we got up to O'Malleys,
Is a thing I'll never know.
We met The Trooper in there,
And we knew he wouldn't blow.

I said could I get the Echo here,
And to me sure he did say.
You'll get one from Milo Regan,
He buys one every day!

the soap box players

We were in Dungravan tonight lad's,
We were never here before.
But I bet that we'll do better,
Then we done in old Rossmore.

We thought that we done good there,
Although the crowd was small.
I wonder did old Cassin,
Know what he was doing at all.

Tonight the English lady,
We liked her from the start.
But a fellow called Mick Regan,
He broke her bloody heart.

Then she cried for poor Mulcahy,
Saying isn't he very dull.
He's kissing Miss McCarthy,
And he grunting like a bull.

Then she said there's another,
An by Christ he makes me sick.
His name it is John Fraher,
The bloody lunatic.

But there was one young man there,
He set my heart on fire.
But he's another idiot,
His name is P. Dwyer.

When she spoke to Hehir the Butcher,
Oh she began to shiver,
Saying if he had a bloody knife,
I swear he'd sell my liver.

She picked out another fellow,
And then she started crying.
Saying Christ I cannot stand him,
And his name is Patrick Brien.

She said the chap called Foley,
Straight away her heart did win,
But she said how could a Bishop,
Come from the bloody glen.

She looked Mick Fraher up and down,
And said he was a wreck.
Straight away she blamed the woman,
He is going with from Bal Bek.

She pointed out one girl,
Saying I don't like her at all.
Ye know the one I speak of,
She's living in Staball.

And when she looked at poor old Madge,
She said she thought twas fun,
To see a crippled woman,
When she started for to run.

And now she said in finishing,
This is what I have to say.
To manage all those idiots,
I pity Kevin O'Shea.

But keep on trying Kevin,
And prove your are no coward.
I know you've one to help you,
The prompter Bridie Howard.

And then S.B.O'Donnell,
He's the greatest of them all.
Ye know that only for him,
Ye wouldn't be there at all.

But still we mean to carry on,
Win, lose or draw who cares.
We'll always stick together,
The good old Soap Box Players.

fishing in kerry

I always will remember,
the lovely month of May.
When our Daddy said dear children,
we will go on a holiday.

Oh we were all delighted,
we laughed we were so Merry.
When he said we'd all go swimming,
In the seaside back in Kerry.

We knew we'd have a great time,
that's one thing that we knew.
So we said to our Mammy,
will we bring poor Granny too.

The first day we were back there,
to catch fish we were all trying.
For Granny went up to the shop,
And got a rod and line.

We lifted all the stones around,
And searched in every nook.
To try and get worms,
That we'd put on the hook.

Then we went down to the water,
Seamus said we'll get one here.
But when he went to fire it in,
It stuck in Granny's ear.

When Granny got the prod,
She opened up her mouth.
And she said I am your Granny,
Do you think I am a trout.

Then Madeline took the fishing rod,
saying I know I am no boy.
But a girl could also catch a fish,
so I am going to try.

There was a man behind them,
what are you doing he said.
When the hook and the big fat worm,
landed up on his baldy head.

Dede said you're doing things all wrong,
with that ye must agree.
I'll show ye how to do it right,
please give the rod to me.

She waved the worm here and there,
Yes things were going grand.
But when she went to fire it ,
It stuck on Mammy's hand.

Her finger it was very sore,
In fact it's sore yet.
She said it was fish fingers,
Dede was trying to get.

Then Barry he picked up the rod,
And he said let ye watch me.
So he fired the hook and worm,
out into the sea.

Then he said I have something,
I think it is a whale.
But when they pulled the line in,
T'was a tiny little snail.

So Granny said we cannot fish,
I think we'll have to stop.
So she picked up the rod and line,
And took it to the shop.

But Seamus said what harm,
we'll catch them all next year.
We will all know how to do it,
For Granda will be here.
(the late James Leahy)

WHO?

Do I know you? Do I know me?, When will reality hit?, We don't know the half of it.

Eamon

Josephine
—

I think theres light
            in everyone,
And some make others shine
Its your gift to hold
                them both,
And make all you touch entwine

Light is the greatest
              gift we have,
Surpassing these earthly grounds
AND I know that all,
        who've touched your soul
will know where it abounds.

———————————

93

the wine-breath

They'd put her in a stark interview room with one window that gave her a view of grime encrusted yellow brick. Now she stared out there until the detective returned to continue the interview, a different female officer accompanying him. She stood behind her, near the door while the man sat in a padded swivel chair at the battered desk.

He'd already informed her of her rights and offered her access to a solicitor. But she'd refused to even speak, shaking her head violently whenever he'd pressed her. His methods had varied - the kindly, fatherly voice - she'd almost succumbed then and laughed - the pleading voice, the menacing voice, as cold and as bleak as that dormitory in which she'd slept during her childhood long years ago.

"Ms Blake," he said now, glancing down at his notes as if to check that he had the correct name, "can you please tell me why you did it? He must have antagonised you - we realise that - and it will make things much easier for you if the case comes to court. You're a respectable citizen and he ... Well you know what he is. If only you'd tell us everything it would help you. We want to help you. You know that, don't you?"

She didn't speak and he continued to press her. His voice took on a whining tone and she shut her ears to it, literally shut her eyes until darkness enveloped her and she was back outside in the world again, entering the railway station where it had happened just hours before - where that thing - that human thing had reminded her too closely of the past...

***

She hadn't actually seen him at first. He'd been hidden from her view by the machine that took instant photographs. The first she knew of his presence was a tug on the hem of her coat. She'd swung around in response and it was then she saw him. He was slumped on the tiled floor, his back against the wall, a bundle of rags with a head sticking out one end, two bleared eyes watching her from an entanglement of black greasy hair.

"A few bob." She was almost certain that those were the very words that had come from that hole which had suddenly opened among the hair - yellow rotting teeth within and a vibrant pink tongue that looked like a new born creature wriggling in its burrow.

She tried to pull away but his grip on her coat was tight - held her shackled. "A few bob." He repeated the words, the eyes pleading, his hand beginning to tremble as he held on. It was only now she noticed his other hand holding the green wine bottle, nails blackened, the skin with the texture of old leather.

94

Did the smell of the wine - that sweet cloying smell - actually reach her nostrils? Did it kill his stench - body sweat, filth, hopelessness - which surely must have clung to him and which she'd certainly become aware of afterwards, mingled then with the stink of fear and blood? Did he actually say: "God bless ya?" Or did she imagine it all?

She saw her own reaction to him mirrored in his eyes as the pleading was replaced by loathing - maybe even hatred. The smell of the wine came to her again, much stronger now, and he spoke once more. She tried again to pull away and his hand brushed against the back of her leg, just above the hamstrings. She jerked as if stung, and the world of the station - the rushing crowds, the rattle of a trolley, and the roar of a train - receded.

***

Now she no longer saw him nor heard him. Now she was a child again, back in the orphanage, another face in her vision, clean-shaven, heavy jowls, pink lips and tongue moving above the square of white at his throat.

"Sweeties?" he was saying. "Sweeties?" handing her the jelly mixture in a brown paper bag. She was sitting on his knee, his podgy hand on her leg, sliding upwards beneath her blue dress. His face was pressed close to her own, his breathing hoarse and rapid, the smell of wine on his breath.

"Our secret." That was what he'd said afterwards, after the trembling that shook his body, had stopped. "Our secret. You must never tell anyone." He'd kissed her then on the cheek, the words "God bless you, my child," wafting to her nostrils once more, the sweet smell of wine.

***

"It was the smell!" The words burst from her lips before she realised it, echoed about the interview room like startled birds.

The detective jerked in response and stared at her. "The smell?"

"Or the words. I don't know. I think he said: 'God bless...' I'm not sure ..."

Maybe she'd never know why she'd lashed out at him, kicking that filthy stinking thing on the ground. And why, as she'd screamed obscenities at him, and the sound mingled with the clink of the bottle on the tiles and the gurgle of the wine, she'd lashed out again and again, aiming at his face. All she knew was that with each squelch of living tissue, she'd sensed herself being cleansed, being raised up to where no one could ever touch her again.

(Vincent McDonnell)

everything

My love, my life, my hopes, my dreams
these were all the things you were to me,
My future, my past, my present, my goals..
or at least that's how it used to be.
My love, my friend, my mentor, my advisor
is what you used to mean.
Why did you leave the way you did?
Why did you hurt me so?
You used to be my everything.

nothing to do

As the afternoon falls
against a grey yard wall,
stands a group of know-it-alls
who know fuck all:
Johnny Once, the brains of the bunch,
he gets his views from Sky News;
Johnny Twice, the man who usually chooses virtue
because he can't afford vice;
and Johnny Thrice, who lost his farm
with the roll of a dice.
The hermit, the coward and the clown.
They say freedom is wasted on a foolish man*,
but these three don't want to be kept down,
that's why they're hanging around devising a plan.
(*Dostoyevski)

one

The power of one, to see and do
The power of one, this one is you
The power of one, is all it takes
The power of one, what a difference it makes
The power of one, is all we need
The power of one, someone to lead
The power of one, can turn us around
The power of one, is not easily found.
(Ciarán Meade)

sorrow

did you see it?........
when the world stood still
and every beating heart stopped
and every breathing lung gasped
while every eye cried.
the monuments felled
by birds from the sky.
knowing their fate
they swooped in anger
to punish the innocent
for deeds they never knew.
three thousand grains of sand
crashed to the rocks an scattered
the dust rose to darken
the skies, and all was silent.
did you see it?

doubt

friends become acquaintances,
fun becomes time consuming,
chores become responsibilities,
flings become relationships,
music's too loud.
parents get proud,
football's a hobbby,
not a sport!
You're too old for that!
Think about your future!
save, don't play,
work, don't sulk,
that's for kids.
rooms become houses,
weekends become workdays.
I guess this is growing up??

. . . . . .

hours of misspent youth

Today, I looked upon a sunrise,
eagerly awaiting the beauty I had seen daily and loved dearly.
But the sun was dark
and I was heart-broken, always
knowing it would never last
but hoping day by day for
the continuous miracle.

Yesterday I walked a field of roses,
teardrops flowing from every petal,
as I gazed and waited for bloom.
But I was pricked by the thorns,
and bled tears, for bloom was
too far away and the roses -
were dying too slowly.

tomorrow I will cross the river
of dreams and wait for perfection
to greet me on the other shore
and if she doesn't show,
I shall not lose hope
for a grain of sand lies
for every tomorrow.

i am sin

the world becomes a simple place,
when boundaries are broken down,
people from two different worlds,
brought together by love of sound;
and angels cry
when we depart,
and devils moan when we're alone,
for God and for our love of sin;
and love, and death, and bitter things,
I pull apart my Angel wings
and sinners we will live
as Kings.

lithium

why did you have to go?
why didn't you say goodbye?
I know you didn't want to leave
and now you're gone, I'll cry -

so I hope that you're at peace now,
I hope you're happy there,
I hope that you can't bleed now
and you don't have a care.

When you think that you're forgotten
and the whole world's movin' on,
just remember who you left behind:
we'll keep singing your song!

misunderstood

Life is given, a gift,
A miracle - a wonder
Something to behold.
A new life is born
into this world -
to have here and to hold.

Life is lived, a burden.
We didn't choose to come -
We couldn't choose our parents -
We couldn't choose our home -
We spend our lives in bitterness,
For all things great and small.
We think we deserve much better.
Pride before a fall.

Life is taken, sacred -
The coffin's convoy past,
Another cross, a rosary said....
Too late now,
For we are dead.
(Gearóid Murphy)

All i ever wanted was to be part of your heart
        And for us to be together, to never be apart
No one else in the world can ever compare
        You're perfect and so is this love that we share
We have so much more than i ever thought we would

I love you more than i ever thought i could
I promise to give you all i have to give
        I'll do anything for you as long as i live
In your eyes i see our present, our future and past
        By the way you look at me i know we will last

Drawing by Joanne Mulvihill

salute to jazz

White eyeballs set in puce faces;
   Peering round the bushes in the dusk
Of an Alabama evenin'.
   The weary strains of the cotton field chant,
Fused with the odour of sweaty labour.

Amid the drowsiness of neon-lights,
   A midnight blues dripping from a muted horn;
Lonely birth-moans in an eerie cosmic stillness.

With love and improvisation;
   The images of an elegant saxophone
And all its glittering frills;
   Gold-dust veiled in a hazy smoke;
The wispy stains of its form,
   Linger in the composition of a reverie.

In rhythmical search of the primal source,
   On cylindrical shells of maple made;
With parched milky-white velum,
   Stretched taut in chrome hoops,
And all fused in an aura of indium;
   As sparkling reflections converge
In elongated stars.

An enraptured clarinet with its bell raised to the stars;
   Long stick of black liquorice with silver braid.
With ripple and flurry in an ornate riddle of arpeggios,
   Soaring up the silver scales like Shelly's Skylark;
Cascading with a mellow woody resonance.

Swinging in airy freedom,
   On a featherbed of rhythm.
With the crisp whispering off-beat kiss
   of lisping and lame foot-cymbals;
And - with its long neck reclining in stately elegance -
   The mumbling and moaning drone
Of an earthy bass-fiddle.

Candy-striped jacket; straw-boater hat;

A hat from the Latin Quarter;
And cloddish suede shoes gyrate,
   In a madcap boogie jive.

The plaintive planetary wail of Coltrane;
   Sheets and flashes of sound,
In a kaleidoscope of mellifluous riffs.
   Painting quaint images of an urban squalor;
Chaos in harmony; and the degenerate beauty
   Of an opiate state.

Transfixed in the rutted orbit of an axis note;
   In creative search of a graceful flight;
Like a fluttering moth buffeting the glass
   Of a lighted window.

With the structure of a careless stride;
   A tinkling piano meandering dreamily
In a listless ballad.
   Reflective as hazy lights,
On a rippled pool at twilight.

The wild husky wail of a tenor-sax
   In a sprawling blues.
With faint weaving riffs, in tones
   Of such tender forlorn yearning.

A sunburst guitar in a Basie boogie,
   With a half-trapped choppy stomp.
Ebony neck; thin brass frets; and inlay of ivory spots.
   Obliquely held in a fuzzy focus,
With the shiver of vibrating strings.

Like chimes on an ocean floor;
   The dull wafting bells of a vibraphone;
In a slow wistful blues,
   With sweet haunting sadness.

Entranced in harmonic and diatonic thought,
   As sizzling cymbals sing a rhythmic song.
Complacent restrained rapture;
   The be-bop cool equilibrium of dispassionate passion.

riverain moods

What splendour; and what a wonderful piece of theatre!
To see - all sweetened by the mystery of distance -
Sleepy trees woven in a haze, over the glittering
Jewellery of rapids, as a muzzy sun

On its mid-morning climb to glory
Struggles through the muddled veil.
And what strange delight! - When reflected
In still water under motherly trees -

Fragile wads of grey cloud drift wistfully
Through a sombre sky; as if spaced
And shaped by a fickle mood;
Like when the wings of joy beat,

In the shadow of a faltering cumbersome
Sadness, or a sudden feeble surge of joy
Suppressed by a heavy heart;
Or see through a sunlit pool

- By slimy reeds - the wavering shadow
Of a beady-eyed trout on the clear pebbled
Bottom; or a scene so enchanted;
When a low-hung urbane moon

Silhouettes the spidery briar on a shadowy
Promontory over a lonely weir.
And in a momentary glance - on a sullenly
Unsettled day that tempts a melancholy mood -

Fine silky threads of squally mist glisten,
As a weary wind rustles the reeds,
And clear bright water shivers in a watery
Sunlight; and as May clouds thicken .

Over the bushy banks, purple berries shine
Dully through a veil of grey drizzle.
The haunting charms of an evening, when
All the heavens are a bizarre wash

Of crimson shades, as the rim
Of the sinking sun is defined in a blinding
Glimmer, over burbling tepid water;
And when dark water glides sweetly under

Drooping trees, and the gnats hang in the last
Lingering pool of the sun's fading rays,
And the stillness of the evening is broken
By the gulp of a feeding trout; sending

Dreamy ripples spiralling out in a gleam
Of soft curling light; like the liquefaction
Of gold; and then, beyond the gloomy banks,
The silent fields stretch away into

A slowly falling veil of dusk, where
The frothy fleece of the hawthorn softens
To the lone chirp of a bird.
And on a day when the summer sun

Is unrelenting in its labour; what a feast
Of sights and sounds to delight a human heart;
As when shining water trickles through slimy rocks,
Under a mottled green bough where a cobweb

Glistens with a ghostly flutter; the nymphs
Glint silver in a mist of sunbeams,
As petals dance on a dazzling swell,
And the water shimmers green in a blinding glare;

Flickering the homely light of its dance
Across the leaves; And while all along
The humming banks, verdant finery dances
A drowsy mesmeric dance in shimmering vapours;

What bliss then! To sit on a bank
Of long sensual grass, in the shade of a broad
Canopy of sun-dappled leaves, where the air
Is full of the silky water - cool feeling

Of well-being; and let the spirit linger
In the lovely twilight of the subliminal
And all its murmuring melodies;
Or wait until midnight when the sky

Is a smouldering velvet, sprinkled with
The glitter of stars, and a full moon
Silvers the tall trees, and shakes concertina-ed
Shadows across the shallows of the water.
(Michael Murphy)

who sheds light

Who sheds light
Upon my small glories
But the ghosts
Of a struggling tomorrow
Where broken amongst you all
My perception
Rises and falls
With words uttered
Fading into the imagination of the past
When all I could ever ask
Of the passing of time
To make simple the rhythm of this life

golden duds

Money for the honey
Jam for the man
Gold for her fingers
Fur to line the baby's pram
Super turbo injection
From workplace to family home
Champagne foam infection
Impetuous to the bone
Like a lavish marble water fountain
Gushing streams of sludge
An overflow of decadence
Declining in the mud
Swept away by an undercurrent
Of glistening golden dud's
Revolving maniacally round the polarity
Of the Bermuda triangle's hub
(Ray Murphy)

back to school

Fuck you.
Fuck your mother.
Get out of my face.
I stand on your face with my boot.
I throw sand in your eyes.
And I spit on your back.
Go to hell, motherfucker.
Burn and rot in the DARKEST DARK PIT.

I am learning and you are teaching.
I am teaching and you are learning.
NO!
There is nothing being learned here!
You are wasting my time and I am wasting yours!
Get a FOKKIN life! Both of us.
(nonny muss)

editor's gloss:

"The single most important contribution education can make to a child's development is to help him toward a field where his talents best suit him, where he will be satisfied and competent. We should spend less time ranking children and more time helping them to identify their natural competencies and gifts and cultivate those."
Howard Gardner, Harvard Graduate School of Education, author of the Theory of Multiple Intelligences.

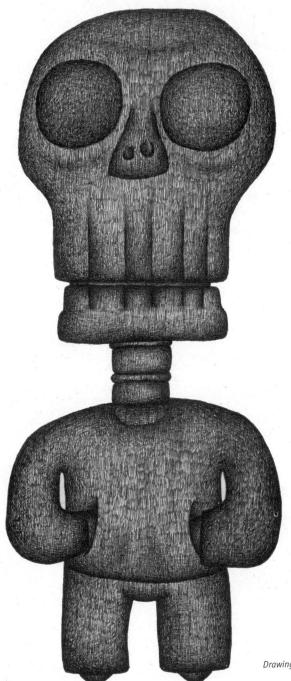

Drawing by Frank O'Sullivan

to arms

Enough of this self-pity,
Their begrudgery saddled my back.
Years of jealousy and envy,
Nailed my arms down.

Why should I feel ashamed?
Is the pursuit of knowledge not honourable?
Is it wrong to desire a sail,
The spiritual power of the sea embraced?

To break a race, you need to break their leaders
Then banish their pride and their ways.
Your nature is inferior, your talents ignorant,
Lie down, or we shall crush you.

Cowardly, ignorant, servile weasel,
Surely death is a release,
To arms, I cry, to arms,
Victory in life or in death.

berlin

The big lumpy backed balloon caravan,
With the marshmallow ears in the sky,
Cavorting around and around with a knife,
And a slice cut down through my eye.

A wafer of sand and a little old man,
Huddling beneath a tree top,
With the laugh of the devil and the dance of a saint,
And a picture of you by my side.

A crispy taste as the teeth crumble,
And a stoke of a brush across wind,
And a red fluffy dog, with a razor sharp bill,
From a window came bounding a pillow.

From darkness grew light, and the anger of god,
Towards hell we drove all the way,
And laughing hysterically, and drawing some more,
Those clouds drew down on Berlin.

the island

It was a dream, a vision of freedom, isolated, alone, untouched by man.
With gulls and seals and cormorants and eels.
The grasses there received no treatment, they flourished.
Aware of my presence the gulls took to the skies,
'Away' they cried, as they shat down on my head.

I close my eyes,
The beach was lit in ethereal summer light,
Wavelets rose and fell along clean, crisp sands,
My boat cut through, and touched the hands of god.

I stood up, and bowed down, an insect in the presence of royalty,
But it welcomed me, and I stayed, my soul shall never part.

the dance

Spear drawn, mask down, fins on,
The predator is released.
Breathing slowly, head moving, sweeping the hall,
Ready.

The lazy dance of Weeds and Algae, as they swayed from side to side,
And the ripples of sunlight, along the sands gave movement to the eyes.

Dogfish!
Safety off, unseen, seen, gone.

The Spider Crabs scurried about the floor as they tried so hard to time,
Their dance with that of the Jellyfish, as the Minnows breezed by.

Fish!
A Wrasse, too far, approach cautiously, silently,
Slight kicks, the Wrasse, through Seaweed disappears.

The Kelp played movements on its bow as the Brittle-Star stood by,
And beheld a tiny Hermit Crab who cared not for ballet.

The predator was moved and touched by all that he had seen,
The music of the oceans, a visceral symphony.

The Wrasse again!
Aim, fire, a hit, the prize of man at sea,
The predator returned to shore, to feast on tender flesh.

The band, unmoved, played on and on, another Wrasse passed by,
And lingered amongst the Weeds, until, a Minnow caught his eye.

113

squirrels

Where are the hazel nuts, where are those trees?
Where are her fruits all gone?
How can a man hope to survive, when all nature's goodness is lost?
How can this be? Where can they be? It's only August right now,
What use are acorns, blackberries and crabs, without a few nuts from a
tree?

Must I root in the soil for a worm and a grub, must I boil nettle soup all the
day?
Do I forage for slugs, and make larvae paste? Oh for the taste of a thistle,
Where are all those sweet nuts gone? I wonder, I wonder.

A squirrel, you fiend, there you go with that nut,
Running so swiftly, so deftly, so free,
There you go with my food and my hopes,
Now my questions are answered, I've learned.

Out here in the woods, where men do not walk, where nature is wild and
free,
I compete not with man, not with law, not with you,
But with squirrels, squirrels, squirrels.

bear hunt, high tatra's

Well now I'm brought down from my roost at the top,
Now I'm brought down to the ground,
Now I've left the city of dreams, to the wilds of reality.

Here I am now, alone in the woods, miles away from police,
I'm on a bear hunt, alone and afraid, where success can lead to destruction.

Where, oh, where can those bears be, perhaps they lie in that vale,
Shall I descend, shall I hike down, shall I become a bear feast?

When your alone, and no longer on top, of the food-chain you see so clearly,
That the eating of flesh, is a natural right, for men and beast equally.

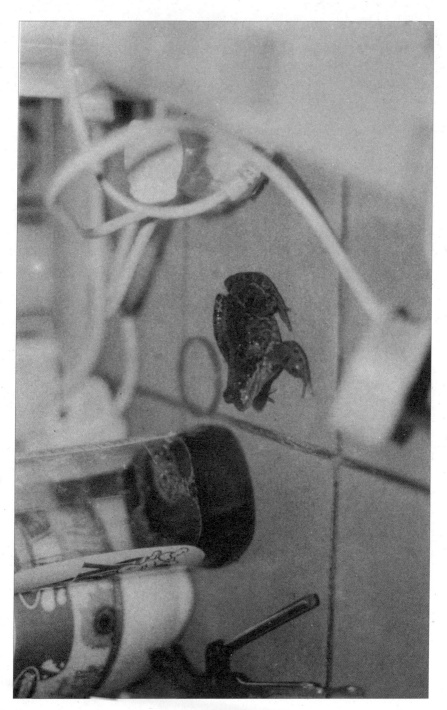

ireland

Where else in the world, does mediocrity triumph,
And excellence is considered a sin,
To flaunt one's skill and decorate one's house,
Is an evil that lurks within.

Where else does the carpenter do a poor job,
To prolong the payments and bills,
And charge a young couple two hundred percent,
So he may spend it on a gill.

Where else do shopkeepers cut their staff's pay,
And threaten and bully their way,
Through deal after deal in fear of themselves,
That as amateurs they'll be exposed as someday.

A human should triumph on effort alone,
And not if the councillor is Aunt Nell,
A system that rewards sloth and ignorance,
Is a system that is destined to fail.

The powerhouse tribes of this planet Earth,
Their heroes are encouraged and trained,
And those that are lesser, are no less valued,
And given their place all the same.

Through effort and blood can man only pass
The test that is set for us all,
To compete with the others, to protect our ways,
To save Ireland from this tragic freefall.

Where else in the world, are the best driven out,
And forced to endeavour elsewhere,
America, Canada, Germany and Spain,
Why must we seek our deserves there.

When the weasels and the Failers,
Drive out the best, and hunt their ideas away,
This country loses, another gains,
And wretched and miserable we'll stay.

So don't hate your neighbour if they have a Merc,
And all you have is a Ford,
Compete with them, don't berate them,
If you deserve it, then you can't fail.

the wind

T'was a great, big wind, that bowled me over and threw my face down in the mud,
And I laughed heartily as my labels were ruined and the muck filled my eyes.
I stood up and walked, straight into a hole, of sink and of wet and of weed,
As the rain pelted down on the nape of my neck, t'was then that the hailstones started.

They battered my skin, and tore at my flesh, and ripped away my frown,
I laughed once again, as I cursed at the sky, and the clouds that were there to torment,
I shouted aloud 'Is there more you can do?' as I stumbled over a ditch,
And fell sideways into briary patch and ripped open my Duck and Cover combats.
I struggled to my feet and caught a cow stare, I said 'How are you today my friend?'
The cow looked away and chewed on its cud and muttered 'Alright sham!'
I glanced over the field and saw a bright light, oh great, the lightening had come,
I started to run, I cared not no more, the rain washed away all the gloss.

I was back to my roots, in the muck and the sink, the city was hosed clean away,
In the muck and the filth, and the shite and the wind, I found my true nature that day.
A hardy man, that will take any weather, that cares not if its hail, rain or snow,
To walk the land, and to feel the fresh breeze, be it force 2, 3 or 8.

"curry ditch"

self destruction

I'll wax my belly with a lump of lard,
Suck carcinogens into my lungs,
No exercise I'll take, sher that would be hard,
And it's way too cold outside.

I'll have an ould can, and slurp on a whiskey,
And I'll put this éclair on my arse,
And if someone says boo, I'll tell them feck off,
Tis my body, I'll do as I please.

Those horrible bastards, with their health and their wealth,
Sher, whats wrong with a KFC,
And when the ould ticker is out of sync,
I'll get a bypass and they'll see.

I'm too old now and too busy to care,
I just want to enjoy life,
You only get one chance to live,
Why would I not treat myself.

Blood pressure 160/100, multiple aortic lesions, heart rate irregular,
Numerous ulcers, including the initial stages of gangrene on the left leg,
The combination of obesity and lack of exercise has resulted in degrada-
tion of the acetabular cup, future hip replacement necessary, not to mention that we haven't scanned the lungs yet, this one's a write off, two years
maximum, and the guy's only 54...........

body and mind

Eat not genetically modified foods, they are engineered to appear healthy
and tasty,
But they lie, they are manufactured to reduce cost, increase productivity.
Eat not machine-processed foods, nature processes it for you,
The art of homeostasis involves balance, upset it, and you will feel ill.

Develop a taste for food that is good, source it, taste it, remember it.
Try not to allow cost to form the basis of what you place in your body,
Food is cheap, beer is not, alcohol is used to kill micro-organisms.
Don't smoke cigarettes, switch to natural tobacco, learn to roll, then quit.

Read books and articles that were written to educate, read not that written
to sell,
Buy a baseball bat and take it to your television, don't try to defend it, just
do it.
Your inadequacies and fears have been implanted onto you by an engineered machine,
You're a fine human being, if a little misguided, didn't you always think
that anyway?

Hike a hill or a mountain, depending on your capability, the views are
breathtaking.
Bring a piece of chocolate with you and eat it up there,
Nothing tastes better than chocolate on a mountain top.
Compare not your performance to other hikers, only to yourself when not
hiking.

Do not compare yourself to other people, you are not other people.

deadline

The deadline draws near,
Anxiety grows,
Decision time again,
Fate has taught me well,
To take on challenges that are difficult,
The greatest rewards to those that prove themselves in battle.

Hope drives the future,
I hope I can perform,
The belly of the beast devours all,
The consumer is a locust,
Do I have what it takes to fire the human race?

Will I be chewed up and spat out, as countries are?
Will I pass opportunities here in favour of false ones there?
I don't think I can take the hardship and the rain much longer.

Why, oh, why do weasels gather around me,
I offer the hand of friendship and they bite it,
Taking all for themselves, generosity and kindness are vices to them,
Where does honour reside?
I have to leave, I have to try, the answers to my questions may await me,
I cannot stay, the weasels attack me daily,
Fighting them off draws too much from me,
Honour has no place in this land.

Columbia

Dreams of the future, the hope of mankind, the exultation of discovery,
Grazing the heavens, the secrets of time, a vessel of evolution.
The driver of life, to expand and to blossom, to build new lives, new ways,
All ruined now, I weep, seven of the finest, seven dreamers of Columbia.
Let there be pain, and sorrow and loss, let there be lessons learned,
And let their memory live on in us, in voyages from mother Earth.

amber

Alone I am, always alone, as I dream,
To be honourable, I must take flight,
And prove myself on the field of battle,
That I am worthy.
Is it better to fight and die?
Than to live alone, away,
Let fear not be a barrier,
To your dreams.
I shall fly, to a distant land, to fight,
Or die in the attempt.

conversations

I hope I can always tell the
way somebody feels
and say something interesting
and always think in my head before
I speak and listen

for the dying/for the terminally ill

The perceived end is actually the beginning*
it's always a beginning
Loads of new beginnings
Maybe it's not too good to know too much
about the new life
except the promise of it
the guarantee
einstein: energy cannot be created of destroyed but only change forms
(*a new beginning)
(Thomas Chrysostomou)

the game

- 'Twas a great game...
-     'Twas...
-     Young Murphy scored two great pints...   .
-     He did...
-     Pity he's such a little arsehole...
-     True...
-     Supposed to take drugs you know?
-     Heard that...
-     Sad really, he's got two lovely parents...
-     'Tis...
-     Course he had to start that fight, ruined the game...
-     He did...

But little did they know, or, more importantly, they choose to ignore the fact that Murphy's parents were two raging alcoholics and Murphy didn't even have any books so he could go to school.
He constantly got cruel beatings and often went hungry for days.
That horrible fucking teacher made little of him because he failed his tests all the time. But how can anyone get A's in something they can't even read about?
The teacher sometimes clattered him for "being smart". Murphy was the hero. He took it all with a smile. Another smart comment and another clatter.

By the time Murphy was 18 he had begun to understand his world. He could sense people's opinions about him.
He started drinking and drinking and drinking, by thirty he got liver failure and died at the ripe old age of 31.

I wonder why?

At his funeral two respectable men sat at the bar speaking to the well respected newly appointed principal deciding the fate of the next generation of youngsters.

bees

Buzzing around shiny street lamps dealing in honey
Enlightening conversations about the power of the euro, the dollar, crowns, apples and even Doves.

A little later the minds awakens and answers
tumble forth to all problems even
those of the world at large.

A little later again and gaping jaws
Depict the sense of loss of honey pumping through the veins.
The body slow and slow now, nothing will do but to find the honey pot and
drop some more.

Before collapsing one bee buzzes:
   "I'm sick of this country, let's all go to England next week.
    I hear they have a Bee Club there."
   "Cool", buzz all the swarm, feeling the worse now.

Friday comes, they swarm to England, buzzing frantically all the way.
Buzzing up through tube stations, trendy bars, around by huge neon lights
and finally the beautiful thumping Bee Club.

The swarm beams and buzzes collectively now, a modern Nirvana, they've
reached the pinnacle.

Seven hours later, the buzzing slows, the night's work done, one bee's
missing though and then, a screaming girlfriend, police and the blue ice
cold flashing lights of an ambulance.
   "He's collapsed, he's blue and sick"
Then the doctor's words:
   "Move dear, he's stopped breathing. One, two, three, four;
    one, two, three, four......."
......one, two, three and four no-more, never again.......

Was it worth it?

sunday night

We had a fine time drinking.
Wine followed by six bottles of cider.
Johnny floored six whiskeys straight then he floored the brother.

The mother's car arrived outside and in come the army of younger brothers: "Come on! She's going mad! You've work. She said your father's going
to kill you!"

"I'm fine," slurps Johnny, "Tell her fuck off. Two pints please Mary when you're ready. Tell him to fuck off too, I'll walk home."

Panic over, Johnny settles back into his rhythm. His sits with half a smile not saying much because he's not really able to. He thinks to himself I feel sorry for Mam but it's not my fault. Sarah dumped me and I have to drink all the time.

At half past three the staggering begins along the crooked mile. His meandering frequently interrupted by small unseen obstacles like lamposts and motor cars.
At the gate he meets the brother squinting at him stupidly in the moonlight and says: "Who did that to your nose? Come on, we'll kill him."
(Paddy O'Donnell)

beyond

Beyond is different from the Otherworld
You'll die to get Beyond but you'll not return from there
The Otherworld on the other hand.
Adjoins our own
It's a world of Gods
Omphalos we travel to in festive times
and taste immortality in joyous peace

Hidden as birds among the branches of shady sycamores
We abandon all earthly interest
Da'wah

pathways

How can I know God without love?
I cant
How can I know God without hope?
I cant
How can I know God without self-surrender?
I cant

I have to learn the symbolism of the twenty-two
I have to learn the alphabet
I have to learn the book
I have to learn the pathways through the leaves.

whisperer

I dream of the dead in all their guises
and curse the half sleep of all of us
I am told to whisper these nightmares
to a hole in the ground
cover it with a stone and they will stop

stolen bed

There is that break in century
Where the marching of armies
echoes through fog fired days
The clatter and whine of track and jeep
pushing forward
intent on new victory
While some poor sod is sound asleep
blissfully dreaming in tomorrow's stolen bed.

shadow

Last night, I met the son of a widow in secret
He again asked me to join
Pledged advantages that accrue
to someone like me
Said that they'd agreed
I belong with them under the fig tree
I told him - no, not yet -
I will continue to trust in my shadow
for the time being

abstract

We all walk through life at times like the poor souls in Plato's cave
Hidden in our loss of things
Spirit-bound in shadowy things
Guessing God's image without colour or frame

Some people even when they get to see the full picture insist
on re-making the whole thing in totally abstract ways.

Tell me are these fucking artists right?

according to Erasmus

The three evils.
The vestiges of the fall are

blindness.
The blindness that impairs our judgement
and leads us into temptation
and condemns the innocent convicts truth
and frees evil from the chained block

The flesh.
The flesh, which corrupts our will
and leads us into temptation
Has us replace spiritual rewards
for lusts folly and illusory happiness
Demoralising ethic and making
a whorehouse of God's temple

And weakness.
The weakness that destroys constancy
and leads us into temptation
Has us doubting truth in Scriptures
Following this false path and that.
Watered down love.

Soldiers as prisoners without having fired a shot.
(Donal O'Flynn)

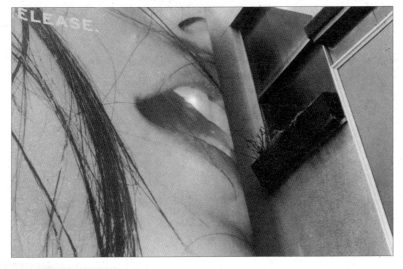

an Irish hope

February 1st 2001

It was a dull wet day. The wind swept shores of Atlor Bay shuddered as the sea sent murky waves spiralling across the earth like sand. A lone figure stood by a large jagged shaped rock, his fierce green eyes scanning the horizon of the bay. "Cherasta", he cried suddenly. Over the horizon came the tall mast of a Spanish galleon. The man watching pulled his mantle tighter around his shoulders. Slowly he looked around, one hand on the sword hilt which was hidden underneath his mantel. He made sure no one was watching him before concentrating on the large galleon which was looming closer every second. As the ship came closer, the man, whose name was Francis O'Toole, thought to himself, how dangerous this was. He had been against the idea since Hugh Roe O'Donnell suggested it, but knowing the risk of taking the Spaniards to Tir Chonaill, O'Toole volunteered to lead them to O'Donnell's castle. O'Toole wondered how O'Donnell was planning to hide the Spaniards from the English, who - he knew - had spies everywhere. The impressive ship dropped its heavy anchors into the dark water by a cave hidden by the huge swell of water, which was filtering through the cave.After a few moments, a wooden boat - able to seat thirty men - was lowered, followed shortly by another. Slowly the boats began to fill with men, and within ten minutes the two boats were making their way towards the shore. O'Toole estimated that between fifty and fifty-five men were in the two boats. The galleon began to pull up its anchors and slowly began to depart Irish water. O'Toole couldn't help noticing the Spaniards looking sadly backwards at the drifting galleon. O'Toole couldn't help feeling a slight sorrow for the men. He couldn't imagine anything worse than dying in a strange country for people whose language you couldn't even speak.

(Denis O'Gorman)

just because i was i am

JUST BECAUSE I WAS I AM
THE PERMANENCE OF MY PAST
THE ACTUALITY OF MY PRESENT
THE REALISATION OF MY FUTURES
THE IMMUTABILITY OF ETERNITY
AN UNENDING LINE OF GALACTIC STARDUST
STRETCHING FROM GOD TO GOD
BREATHING IN AND OUT
ALTERNATING, CHANGING, MUTATING.

EACH SPECK AND GRAIN PERFECT
WITH SUNLESS VOIDS LIKE VACANT FIELDS
AWAITING THE SEEDING STARDUST
OF OUTLIVED GALAXIES
RENEWING, REFORMING RELIVING
ALL OF THE PASTS
ETERNITIES OF PASTS INTERMINGLING IN THE HOLOCAUST OF REBIRTH
IAM.

raging storms tearing at my sanity

RAGING STORMS TEARING AT MY SANITY
TREACHEROUS LOGIC, ILLUMENED FANTASY
VISION OF DARKNESS
RECOLLECTIONS OF YESTERS' PURITY.

DAUNTING TASKS UNDONE
IN THE NARROWING TUNNELS OF THIS CATACOMB.
WIDE AWAKE, STARING BLINDLY BLANKLY
NO FUTURE, NO WAY OUT, NO WAY IN
THE FEAR OF TERMINATION.

HOPE'S LIGHT FLICKERS
FAITH IN AN AFTERLIFE,
CHILDHOOD'S BRAINWASHING.
FANTASIES OF GHOSTLAND

FLOWING RIVERS OF EVERCHANGING FACES
THAT WAS? HE? WHAT?

CLOUDS OF DISEMBODIED DESIGN
UNFOLD. VIOLENCE IN SLOW MOTION
UNTOUCHABLE UNREACHABLE.

LIFT THIS CHOKING CLAUSTROPHOBIA
RELEASE ME FROM THIS
PAINFUL DISTRESSING AUTOPOSITIONAL GAOL.
I DESIRE FREEDOM.
(John F. O'Regan)

irish winter

When icicles hang on the wall - and logs for the fire are drenched wet in the hall,

When birds no longer sing on the wall,

When your front garden is a blanket of snow, and you ruin the pattern if you walk through,

When animals no longer graze but need to be fed lots of straw,

When your skin cracks from the cold,

When you wish you were a bird able to fly to pastures new, and return in the spring of life,

When there is an 'r' in the month and you sow shrubs from your neighbour's garden hoping for new life in the New Year.

dancing

Music, men,
Waltz, Jive,
Drink, Stink,
Separated, Married,
Kids, Age,
Affairs
Choice....You have a choice....use it...

christmas

How did you get over it?
Did you go anywhere?
What did you get?
I got over it,
I didn't go anywhere,
I got nothing....

Petal

Mottle - black, brown with highlights of gold
Paws, claws, Miaow...
Flies, birds, mice,
Run and play.

mart

Cows, Pigs, Donkeys, Hay
Stalls bright and gay
Egyptians with their wares
Irish with their cares
Selling their cabbage, spuds, carrots, parsnips, - in season.
Apples.
Faces weathered from life.
Character lines of a life spent.
Women with their hair nets
Selling their fowl
?Are you all right Ma'am - would you like some geese.
Outside - bales of hay.
Another load, hope they sell it all today.

Drawing by Joanne Mulvihill

first night
You call me up
I say Hi!
You speak of your migraine
Curtains - closed all day - dark room -
You left in a hurry - your needs were not met.
You tried, you felt, you said ?would you blame me.
Is said they cost me nothing - eau naturelle
I do not give in - I push you away -
Even though you make me feel good...
I will please myself later...

4th January
Walk, admire, distance, and spire
Trees, houses,
All dressed in white
View sunset
Home alone..

(no title)
I want to go there
Take me
Make me
Feel me
It's Ok
We are one

past
Reflect, forget
Cancer of life
Valley of tears
Move on, sail...
Be free...

room
Lilac - white - ceiling bright
Bulb bright
Curtains, pink, grey, net
Glass - look - see
Wardrobe of life
Door - protect - shelter
My room
Noise - radio....feel good

friday night
Friday night is my night
It's easier she said
Keeps things in a pattern
Petite, dainty, glasses, old.

cobwebs
Cobwebs - are they a sign? Are you with somebody else
You are not absolute
You need to be cleansed
You do not deserve me...................GO..................
(Anne "P")

the china cabinet

It was just a ring, a small heart-shaped signet ring with my initials engraved on the top and "Always and Forever" inscribed along the inside band.

I stared at my daughter as she sat with her hands beneath her knees, rocking back and forth, crying large sorry tears. "I'm sorry Mom, I'll find it, I promise." But it was gone and I walked away from her and didn't hesitate when she called "Mommy' her baby name for me.

Later I found her asleep across her bed, her shoulders still shuddering from the interminable crying. I slipped off her shoes and pulled the blankets over her. As I lifted her, her arms, still small, crept around my neck and she held me near in her sleep. Sitting there in the dark with her, loving her again, I thought for the first time in many years of Mrs. Griffin.

****

Visiting at Mrs. Griffin's house was a brand new experience every time. Visits were by invitation only, irregular, and with very little notice. They were issued in person and as far as I remember my mother was not consulted about the convenience of the time or date chosen.

She was old, ninety or a hundred we guessed, and seemed to be round all over. Her hair was silver gray; very long, braided and wrapped in perfect circles on top of her head where it was pinned with what seemed to be a million clips. Her face was round, with cheeks like a chipmunk, her skin hung loosely on either side of her face, and her eyes were blue, shining like a special marble. She wore a gray, habit- like dress, the only variation being a floral cotton apron that hung from her neck and was secured around her waist by two large ties. She spoke with an accent, English I think, and it seemed to add to her already strong air of authority.

She lived with her husband Percy. He didn't speak very much because he hated children, we were told. Years before he had an accident with his eye and if the rumours were true the socket behind the closed lid was empty. Somebody once told us that his first wife stuck a knitting needle through his eye because he was mean to her and wouldn't let her have children. He spoke, rarely, with an accent also. He didn't really have much to do with us.

When we arrived for our visit we rang the doorbell and waited. Sometimes the door opened immediately, other times we waited five even ten minutes. When Mrs. Griffin opened the door, she looked at us through the screen, smiled and the day began. The living room was dark, and it took our eyes a while to adjust to the difference. The room was filled with old wooden furniture with patchwork cushions thrown about. The wood floors were covered in varying degrees by handmade cotton braided rugs; the amount of floor visible decreased as she added new strips to the rugs. Mrs. Griffin's things and Percy's invisibly divided the room. Everything on the left side of the room belonged to her and everything on the right to him. The two never mixed. Percy's side consisted of a large stone fireplace with small wooden shelves built into the stone. Each shelf held an ornament. On either side of the fireplace was an armchair; Percy sat to the left, and was usually reading.

In Mrs. Griffin's part of the room, which was bigger than Percy's, there was an armchair with a long couch beside it. In neat piles were the different things that she needed at hand: her sewing box, her recorder and whatever book she was reading at the time. At the far end of the room stood a large piano. Once when I was a novice I opened the lid and began to bang on the keys making what sounded to me like beautiful music. Mrs. Griffin appeared at my side and without a word removed my fingers from the faded ivory and closed the lid. She stood over me and looked into my eyes for what seemed an age and said " The piano is not a toy, it is a musical instrument and deserves the respect you will give it."

Every visit had a routine. An invitation for lunch was the exception to the rule, only one of us was invited at a time. The time was always one o'clock and the menu never varied: toasted cheese sandwich and a glass of milk. I don't remember ever asking for or having more than one sandwich: I do remember savouring every bite. The table was always set for two. Percy never joined us, and Mrs. Griffin sat with me and talked while I ate. She didn't have a sandwich simply a cup of tea. "When you grow up you must go to England, then you will see civilized living. The men are so tall and handsome, so gallant. Yes such a civilized society, not like this country, a bunch of savages." I nodded as I ate my lunch promising myself that I would go some day and see this Camelot she described.

On Sunday morning at we served breakfast to Percy, using the ornaments in the fireplace. One of the ornaments was a tiny cast iron frying pan with a flat stone inside that we decided was an egg; another ornament was a small brass coffeepot with matching doll size cups. Percy sat in his chair reading and we would ask "Well Percy how would you like your eggs, sunnyside up?" He would look up from his book and roar "Bina, Bina, get them out of her, get them away from me." With the final roar we ran as fast as we could out to the porch and collapsed into fits of petrified laughter.

Some days when she was feeling tired we sat on stools in front of her armchair with our knees touching and she told us stories. She sewed as she talked, holding out a thread occasionally to the person allocated the scissors to cut. She showed us how to take apart and clean her recorder; she explained how precious her piano was to her; she showed us her arthritic knees and the swelling we couldn't see. Everything had a lesson. She used to say, and although we didn't understand what she meant we remembered, "Girls listen to me: always own your own hammer, then if you want to hammer a nail you can hammer it."

The musical instruments taught us respect for creation and beauty; the jigsaw puzzle that we all did together taught us patience; the rules about everything were for discipline. The rules in Mrs. Griffin's house were clear and could not be broken. One time, I remember, she had a small orange tree growing in the living room in a pot. She explained that they were delicate plants and needed a lot of care and that too much handling would kill them.

Every visit we would rush to the tree to see if any oranges had come out yet. One day we nearly burst with delight; there, barely the size of a small berry was a tiny orange. It grew and grew until it was the size of a ping pong ball. It looked just like a miniature orange, and the temptation to feel it overwhelmed me one day until I reached out and as gently as I could felt the skin. The tiny orange dropped off the tree into my hand. Paralyzed, I looked at it sitting there in my hand and I closed my eyes in the hope that this was a nightmare. I tried everything to get the orange to reattach itself to the branch to no avail. Oh my God what was I to do? I carefully placed the orange on the earth in the pot and hoped that Mrs. Griffin would think that it had fallen off because it was ripe. I moved it from side to side but through my guilty eyes I knew it didn't look like it had just fallen off. I knew what I had to do. I picked the orange up very carefully and placed it in the palm of my outstretched hand and walked out onto the porch where Katy and Mrs. Griffin stood talking. Katy saw me first and when she saw the orange sitting in my hand her hand flew to her mouth. Mrs. Griffin turned and looked first at me then at my offending offering. She didn't say anything. Tears came to my eyes, "I'm so sorry, I didn't mean to damage it, I just wanted to feel it to see if it felt like a real orange, I tried to stick it back on but it wouldn't ..." this last word came out as a sob. Mrs. Griffin carefully removed the orange from my hand and said quietly "I'm glad that you were honest enough to tell me yourself. Katy take her home." And she turned her back and we were dismissed. Katy wouldn't stop talking about it: she was annoyed because she thought we wouldn't be invited again. I was beside myself with misery until the next invitation came and it did come the following week. Mrs. Griffin never mentioned the incident again, and I was the model visitor for a long time to come.

****

Everything in Mrs. Griffin's house had a story attached to it, it seemed. Downstairs in her basement she had a workshop. The walls were covered with pegboard where tools of all descriptions hung in rows. In the centre of the room was a large workbench with bits and pieces of different machines and household appliances in varying stages of dissection. She taught us about the different tools and tried in vain most of the time to explain the basic theories of ......'Girls heed me now, learn how things work. If you know how they work you can fix them when they break.' Mrs. Griffin had a way of speaking that had a mesmerizing effect. When she told us about her china she seemed to reach a different, nearly spiritual, level.

The china cabinet stood in the dining room. It was a three cornered two level cabinet. The bottom half was enclosed by two doors, the top part was glass and displayed various pieces of china and crystal. Mrs. Griffin removed every piece of china and crystal every week, piece by piece, to clean them. If we were there on a cleaning day she made us sit at the far end of the dinning room table, far away from the china, and we were forbidden to touch any piece of it. We had limited access to most things in her house, once we had demonstrated our ability to treat them with respect, but the china was absolutely forbidden.

Every piece was more precious to her than the next. Her tea set was from England and was "fine bone china"; it was a wedding present from her mother. The set was so delicate, with tiny red roses on each side of the cups and saucers; it didn't seem possible that the handles could bear the weight of the cups. The crystal glasses and goblets seemed to have tiny lights embedded in them that created blue and white designs on the walls and ceilings when the sunlight fell on them. Each glass had a story. Mrs. Griffin had waited and waited for the day when she would have dinner parties and display her beautiful crystal. She described the table setting to us over and over and as she polished the glasses and carefully replaced them in the cabinet her face changed and she became silent. She forgot us for a time until every piece was safely stored and the key turned in the lock and place on top of the cabinet. When she was finished we went back to the living room where she planned menus and guest lists. We believed her and hoped that when the day came for the dinner party we would be invited to attend.

On a rainy day in August we sat on our stools in front of Mrs. Griffin as she sewed and we talked about this and that. One particular addition to Mrs. Griffin's fascinating objects was a pinking shears. It was heavy to hold and difficult to cut with but it occupied us and she would give us turns to cut paper or scraps of material. She had promised to get it for us that day but sometimes she forgot things, and we had to wait until her story was finished to remind her - it was rude to interrupt. I knew that the pinking shears was on top of the china cabinet because it peeked out over the edge. Maybe, I thought to myself, if I get it and put it by her side she will think it was there all the time.

Slowly I got up and went to the dining room. The china cabinet was so tall that I knew I couldn't reach the scissors without some help. I thought about using a chair but if I made a noise that would be the end of that and we would be sent home. I opened the doors on the bottom of the cabinet and placed one foot on the shelf to see how sturdy it was, it seemed just fine. The glass doors on top were locked and I needed something to hold on to; the only thing I could see that could possibly help me was the key sticking out of the lock. It was small and I would have only one chance to swing around, knocking the scissors to the floor but I felt it could work. With one foot on the shelf I lifted my other foot from the floor by pulling myself up with the key and was suspended briefly in this position before I felt the cabinet move. Clinging tightly to the cabinet, my feet now hanging in mid air the cabinet, with me firmly attached, fell forward and crashed to the floor.

As I lay underneath the china cabinet, with Mrs. Griffin's china and crystal in splinters about my head, I found the weight comforting. For a while I forgot what had happened until I heard the footsteps above my head. There were three pairs: Katy's sandaled feet, Mrs. Griffin's black canvas shoes and Percy's slippered feet.

All three stood still for a while and then I felt the weight lifted from my chest. Percy bent beside me and gently lifted me from the floor and held me in his arms, "Are you hurt?" he asked checking my head for cuts. I couldn't speak. I turned and looked up at Mrs. Griffin; she stood looking at the floor, rocking back and forth her eyes fixed on the splintered glass around the floor. Katy stood at her side, pulling at her sleeve - she did not move. I turned my head into Percy's chest as he held me. Eventually he stood me up and brushed the glass from my clothes and hair, I felt unsteady as I turned to Mrs. Griffin. She had not moved, but had begun to cry.

I walked over and stood in front of her trying to think of something to say but nothing came out. Finally Percy guided me to the front door with Katy by my side and said that he would talk to my mother later. I wasn't afraid of what my mother would do, it didn't matter.

I was relieved when she died. She tried in a vague way to pretend nothing had changed but she didn't convince me. I felt awkward with her. She didn't address me directly and although she didn't exclude me I was excluded. She didn't tell us stories anymore because there were no stories, the china had been the story. I cried and prayed that God would find a way for her to forgive me but the truth was that it wasn't me Mrs. Griffin couldn't forgive it was herself.

My daughter was sleeping soundly now and I knew in the morning she would forgive me and we would be just fine.
(Sheila Quealey)

my letter

(The following could have been written by Jimmy 'Weeshie' Murphy, R.I.P.
who died recently. Self-explaining to anybody from Charleville.)

No longer you see me on your street,
Standing in a doorway with a bottle by my feet,
For winter's too harsh to just carry on,
To a much better place I'm now gone.

My life I've lived well, one day to the next,
I didn't do much but what I did was my best,
And when I was young and with some strength to spare,
I'd work with the farmers for their tea and good fare.

My sin, if I had one, was the great sin of pride,
I didn't look posh, but I felt great inside,
For the drink kept me warm, kept away colds and flu,
And sure I was happy, maybe happier than you.

If those whom I've hurt were to shout-out right now,
It's silence you'd hear like a nun with a vow,
My friends, they were few, but a few who did care,
My loved one's are one, the dry warm air.

If thanks I must say it's for your food and your drink,
For your prayers by my coffin, I'd wish I could wink,
For your drive through the town to my last place of rest,
In Holy Cross, oh, my God, I'm as good as the best...

to Shakespeare

Oh, Bard of Avon, your name synonymous with words and rhyme,
Your twisted phrases explained to simple minds and mine,
Your plays and sonnets bring fear of amnesia ------forgetfulness,
Our fragile minds not comprehending your slang and craftiness.

Our teacher, at the lectern, glaring at those who look silent,
His golden cane hangs like a whip from his belt, oh I relent,
And say I can't recall that line, "yon Cassius has a lean and hungry look,"
Back home on the farm the dogs and calves have everlasting charm, ah
fuck.

He moved towards me, skirting all others, cane swishing through the air,
I'm asked ---oh shit, I'll die today of pain and shame, it's not fair,
Why me, you long rat with yellow hair, that cane your only power,
Mostly I'm a happy lucky lad but your glare makes me dower.

Can't remember, my head's blank, my hand out to take the blow,
Soon the raised red stripes across my palm will glow,
The flesh beneath my skin will boil somewhere between wrist and finger-
tip,
The golden cane hangs from it's bent end from the belt at his hip.

Back at the lectern, he smiles to himself, glad, I think,
My digits ache and glow with pain, our teacher smiles - a gink,
It's all your fault, old man of Avon, long verses rhymed, forgot,
Not bard but bastard, you and your cottage, I wish you'd rot...
(I hated English and he caused most of the problems)

street walker
Oh, I remember clearly,
When our streets were made of mud,
And the horses on the sidewalk,
Made puddle, like only horses could.
And every where you tried to walk,
You stood on horse's shite,
For keeping clean was difficult,
No matter how you try it.

The years went by and concrete came,
Our town looked clean and new,
Our streets were swept and washed with rain,
And horses they were few,
But with the concrete came the car,
You see them old and new,
One person drives them,
And sometimes have a crew.

The years have slowly gone,
And now I am fifty older,
And cars left on the street, that's fine,

Or on the wide hard shoulder,
But parking on the footpath - no
My zimmer frame won't fit,
'Twas easier with the muddy streets,
And the heaps of horses shit.
(Before Urban Renewal and the advent of Traffuc Warden - parking was disastrous - and the above came to mind.)

it's time to write

(A young lad's loneliness in a far away place.)
Many weeks now gone, it's time to write
I had a lovely trip, a smashing flight.
The food is good and the drinks just fine,
But Ma, the bread is Hard.

Found work, Day one, I'm digging holes
The local lads are standing poles,
The heat is mighty, like red-hot coals,
But Ma, the bread is hard.

There's fellows here with names diving,
And skin so black it has a shine,
And when their talking, I neer hear mine,
And Ma the bread is hard.

On Sunday morning just after mass,
I met this lovely, blondy lass,
Her Ma cooked lunch, that was a gas,
But Ma, the bread was hard.

We rise up at the break of day.
Working long but there is hectic pay,
And the dollars in my pocket stay,
But Ma, the bread is hard.

When I left home I made a vow,
That one day, somewhere, somehow,
I'd buy my ticket back, that time is now,
For Ma, the bread is hard.

the visit

(I now live on a site once occupied by Kitt and Dor, two local characters around Killmallock in the '50's and '60's)

Was ere last night or the night before
That two dear souls came to my door
'Twas Kitt and Dor, I knew them well
"We're here from heaven, never went to hell"
"Come in," said I "and take a seat
You're looking well, no cloven feet."
They looked me right into my eye
Hadn't seen me since I was a boy
"Oh" says she "Were you in bed"
"Not at all " said I think I too was dead.
Into our kitchen they both came
And sat beside the fire. "No crane"
Sad Kitt, "What have they done
To the house I lived in and had such fun"
"The roof fell in and the walls fell too
And in this house we've an inside loo,
And thank you Kitt for this piece of land
The house we live in is simply grand."
As Dor stood up, Kitt said to me
"We'll lift him up so he can see"
We fixed a chair by the window wide
So he can see out from here inside
"Where are all the little streets" he thought
Where as a boy I played and fought
And drank black porter and had my fill
T'was a small few pence in Maggie's till.
I see the ruins of times gone by
And the monks all gone, oh, I could cry
And in the place where most will rest
The crows fly through the windows crest."
With gentle care we brought him down
And on his wrinkled face, a frown
For had he wished he hadn't come
To his place of youth and boyhood fun
And as the tears came to his eyes
A shrilling sound, a piercing noise,

The blasted clock did ring,
My dream was gone, the silly thing
Alas, another day had come
And whom do we remember, all are gone.

radio

"Don't touch that knob," my father said,
Glaring through me, with his hand raised to his head,
Surely, I thought, it was no great wrong
To find another station, that played a different song.

But radio was this magic thing to look at and to hear,
Sure, to move the know just slightly was the cause of greatest fear,
For single "dongs" and mono tones announced that start of the day,
O Donnell Abu, to work and the angelus to pray.

The news brought stories from far and wide,
At excitement and disasters we often laughed and cried,
And word from places so far away we'd never heard their names
And we would shout and clap on Sundays, to hear our native games.

'Twas Joe Linnane with questions, we always wished for more,
And Din Joe, with music and with dancing, on the weekly take the floor,
But Sean Og on Sunday night, brought silence to our home,
We'd wait up to hear whom we'll meet next, was it Dolla or Shinrone,

And racing was a joy to hear, O'Hehir talked horses past the post
While we checked our betting dockets to see who won the most,
Old Eamonn Kelly told us stories of ghosts and ghouls of yore,
While with eager ears we listened for a noise outside our door.

The anthems played last thing at night to end our weary day,
Our radio was the great companion that helped us along the way,
I'd dare not touch that sacred thing, 'Twas high upon the hob,
For the radio had a pride of place, as had that precious knob.
(poems created by P.J. Russell)

fading flame

A man, a hero
A fighter with a sword
Who would die for his country
Than be bribed or disloyal.

Spice, he believed,
Had numbed his brain.
Treason and malice
Were not part of his game.

Influential and devilish
A woman would you believe
Unsexed with ambition
Called darkness for the deed.

"It's great, I'm King,
But happiness is gone.
The candle flame is fading
My life is nearly done."
(Ian Ryan)

Photograph by Deirdre Sheehan

mount russell

Mount Russell, Mount Russell, away from the hustle,
And bustle of the modern day life.
You're my little bit of green, my beautiful mountain scene,
And I will love you for the rest of my life

Mount Russell, Mount Russell, with your valleys and your trees,
The splendour of your beauty brings me to my knees.
Forever I'll bless the day I came your magic way
And your peace cleansed my body and my soul

Mount Russell, Mount Russell, you're so wild and so free,
With your sisters beside you, you spell liberty,
Unscarred and untouched throughout history,
Embracing and gracing the locality.

Mount Russell, Mount Russell, you've mended my heart,
From your hills and your people I hope never to part.
You stand so proud and tall and you hear me when I call,
You will always be my true Irish home.

castle oliver

Castle Oliver you stand encircled by your land,
Though not so much now as once long ago.
Proud you still are with your turrets so high,
Your rooftops reaching up into the sky.

Commissioned by two ladies ahead of their time,
Elizabeth and Mary of Scottish line.
Gascoine and Oliver, the last names of these two,
We owe them our thanks for creating you.

You look to the mountains over fields of green,
From all of your windows there's a beautiful scene.
For each day of the year there's a different view,
To watch the seasons ever changing hue.

What parties have you seen, what tales could you tell,
Of those who for a while in your walls did dwell?
Who dined at your tables, who danced at your balls,
Whose laughter has echoed through your marbled halls?

Tell the names of the maids who've bobbed and curtseyed
And the glamorous ladies who've dimpled and flirted.
Who's hidden in your shadows, who's climbed your stone stairs,
Who's knelt in your bedrooms to say their prayers?

Many the lovers who've kissed beneath your trees,
How many suitors have fallen to their knees?
And while others inside have blissfully slept,
Who's were the footsteps that illicitly crept?

The walls around you, built when labour was cheap,
For a penny a day, many earned their keep.
Little enough, but it kept them from famine,
And the fear of the workhouse door from slamming.

So much history, blood and sweat have you seen,
Loved by many, both orange and green.
For four hundred years of Ireland's past,
Castle Oliver you were made forever to last.

Cruel has been some of your fate,
Pillaged and plundered to a desolate state.
Torn and mistreated, you've wept your own tears,
As sombrely you've withstood those darker years.

But people who love you, live in you now,
And slowly but surely, someday somehow,
Every part of you will tell it's own story,
As you are restored to your former glory.
(Fran Stone)

15th birthday

Precious, precious child, where have you gone?
Do not hide, come back to me.
Come back, child, I need you.
The child never returned.
I died that day.
I stopped believing,
Falling into emptiness,
Stumbling deeper and darker
Into NOTHING,
Suffocating through and through,
Over and over, slower and slower.
Endless screams echoing through my soul
Haunting every thought, choking every word
Every breath. I cut deeper.

I was a child. Why wasn't I left untouched?
Creator of pure unfiltered thoughts,
Master of my imagination,
Wizard of magic and mystery,
All has been destroyed.

Where there are people
There is destruction.
Where there is a child
There is a rapist.

out of misery (short and sweet)

Why O Why
Does it always rain on me?
For I am the most depressed in the world.
Why O Why
Has everyone left me alone?
For I am the most depressed person in the world.
Why O Why
It just seems there's no point living anymore.
For I am the most depressed in the world.
Why O Why
Won't you just put a gun to your head
and shoot yourself.

forlorn

Lingering bloody red, piercing yellow twisting
  with raging burning orange.
Awakening blue entwining with my soul.
Why don't you feel the pain I feel?
You were frightened, you left,
I kicked you down into the gutter.
I muttered "Die, you fucker!
Die, die, die you motherfucker".
I welcomed death upon you.
My most dearest, nearest friend.
I am sorry.

But where were
you when I was
lost?
Where were you
when I needed you
the most?
Burrowing in a
sleepless cry
A forgotten
always, you and I,
Like water
bubbling from a
silver jar,
Like the rose that
never died.
It can't rain all the
time.
Will you jump
when I say when?
Will you breathe
out, so I can
breathe in?
How long I've wait-
ed here for you,
OUT OF MY HEAD.
(Elisabeth
Sullivan)

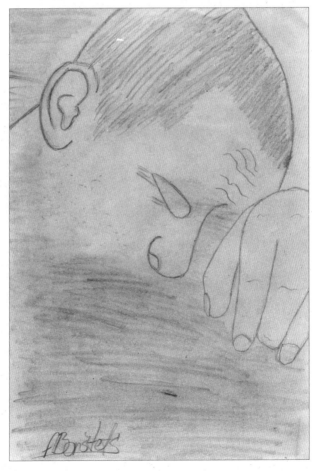

letter written in 1941 to joe grant R.I.P.
from jimmie tuohy R.I P.

Dear Joe
Well here I am again to say
That everything here is rosy.
I got your letter just today;
Twas good to hear from Josey.

I hope that you are keeping well
In dear old London town.
I'm playing soon for Colmanswell
And letting old goals down.

Nothing here has changed much since
I wrote to you last time.
I'm trying to save a couple of pence
To buy some Xmas wine.

Mickey Delaney said to say
That he often thinks of you
And when at night he kneels to pray
His knees get black and blue.

My girlfriend, her name is Joan,
Is very fond of you,
And if and when you do come home
She'll spare a kiss for you.

The porter at Tom Regans
Is still the best in town.
'Tis drunk by all the pagans
In this here crazy town.

Our hurling team is not so good
They never win a game.
They're far much better gobbling food
Or chasing after dames.

But after Xmas he'll be back
That man of great renown.
Ring will play in our attack
And we'll win the hurling crown.

Michael Geary, I am told,
Delivers milk no more,
But soon again it will be sold
By Joe from door to door.

Old Smiths Lane is not the same
Since Joseph sailed away,
And Morrissey's staff can have no game
For Joe's not there to play.

But back again to his old friends
Our Joseph comes again,
And he'll drive us all around the bend
And drive us all insane.

And when in Geary's yard he'll stand
And in Tom Regan's too,
We hope he'll stay in Ireland
We really hope he do.

Well, that is all for now, dear Joe,
Until again you write.
I hope that you will let me know
If I have won that pint.

This letter is a poem, you know,
And it may be a little screwy.
'Twas written to a Grant called "Joe",
From his auld pal Jimmie Tuohy.

Submitted by Geraldine Tuohy and Marie Grant, (daughter).

now I understand my purpose in life........

Mon, 24 Feb 2003 20:16:16

Yes,I am the son of God, where God is the earth, the moon, the sun and the stars, and my mission in life is to spread the wondrous news that joy and wisdom stems from the pursuit of knowledge, in effort and endeavour, the unwillingness to accept failure, the freedom in independence from man (especially the Berty-ites), the futility of greed, the rejoicing in thought and meditation, the purging of negative ions from ones body and mind, the unification of being and spirit in the exploration of the cosmos, send me to space, so that I may travel with my brothers through the wondrous eternity of life and hope, ah, now I understand my purpose in life, and I never even had to take any hallucinogenic chemicals!!!! Its so clear, all religions throughout the world preach the same message, chill out dude, excess is bad, knowledge and wisdom is good, purge negativity, embrace positivity, music, art, poetry, life, life, life.

I shall let my thesis alone now, and instead write my book, I think I'll call it the Book of Life,

and it will be about ze scientific applications of ze ions of positivity into the animal zat is man.....

We are animals, behave as so, that's where it all went wrong, some idiot fucker one day said, 'I don't want to hunt today'. That was the root of all evil. He would not, therefore, others had to work harder to keep the tribe alive, because one would not be responsible for what he was. Then, others got pissed and said, I aint sharing my food with you, my son died today catching that buffalo, I'm gonna put a door on my cave and if you come near it, well fuck you, here look, I'll use this spear on you muthafucka, so then the

tribe split after Bertie said 'Come with me and I promise you everything', he preyed on the weak, used lies and deceit to further his own ambitions, and declared war on the others that shunned him, and they, dismayed, shored up their dwellings, sharpened their spears, and prepared for war. And 'tis that very war that continues today.......

Are you doing something that is positive and healthy and adds value to the life experience, or are you falling further and further into the horrifying oblivion of greed, corruption, sloth and vice. Shiat, shiat, shiat. That's all you have to do. Maintain positive experiences, try to eliminate negative ones. And forget

about what they want you to do. Do what you want to do........ and all you gotta do is make sure it doesn't fuck anybody else up...

Oh yeah, if you fail at something, it means you're either not suited to it or you didn't try hard enough. It has absolutely nothing to do with the horrible, negative concept 'you are a failure.' This is a term that is used by the misguided to hurt you and make you feel inadequate, preying on your emotions so you will end up buying their crap products to make you feel better. Or else it's because they themselves view themselves as failures and do not want you to succeed, because they will feel worse, its horrible, its

horrible, horrible, horrible, ahhhhhh, let me back out to sea..........
If somebody says something negative about you as a person, what they are actually doing is saying, 'I feel like shit', therefore they probably need cheering up on some level. Yes, that makes sense. Instead of saying 'Fuck you motherfucker' and instantly doubling the amount of bad energy, you need to try, to try to say something positive, damn, its very hard when you are Irish. Very hard. We can't express positive emotions very well, damned invaders, drove away our what's the word for that thing......

I need to tattoo something like 'Strength and Honour' onto my body, so I never forget......... shiat, if I'm right, then i never can forget....... There's nothing wrong with humans behaving like animals, what's wrong is humans not behaving like animals, like an animal that is always hunting and never playing or chilling out with its homees is a fucked up animal. Or an animal that is not protecting its offspring or tribe is fucked up. Balance, balance, balance, without out it you get vibrations which inevitably lead to failure, balance, balance, balance, balance........

Anyway, I go now maybe somebody print this out and in ten or twenty years time somebody say to me "Do you remember when you said this?" Jesus I'm bonkers.

sea-kayaking with the Sun-God......

Mon, 24 Feb 2003 13:47:26
This is amazing, I did a lap of Courtmacsherry Bay yesterday, first time out on the sea all winter, apart from the surfing. It was beautiful day, I cursed the swell, sun and wind on my way out, but they were at my back on the return, so the last 5K were fantastic, plus there was a tern just hanging out on the water doing his own thing as I paddled by and I said, 'Hey dude, what are you up to?' and he just looked and me and turned away, saying nothing.... I think he was doing his own thing and had no interest in a stupid human in 17foot of fibreglass.
Then I landed, invigorated. Dizzy from euphoria. So I took a puff of the

gange to calm down. I believe that my body soaked up the positive ions of the sea and transcended my electromagnetic field to create the feeling of euphoria that I am accustomed to after a nice trip on a sunny day. I realised last year that I can't go to pubs after these trips. One night last summer I went to Goughs, met a good man that works in construction industry, and said something like, 'Woah man, I was out on an island last night, I'm off my face from the sea'. He looked at me as if to say: 'You're on drugs'. And I wasn't the one drinking. But I forgot this lesson as it was 5 months since my last trip. Then last night, I went to E***'s gig in their pub.

I tell you at the start I was buzzing, the music was great, then I had 1 pint, the music stopped, I inhaled the carcinogens in the atmosphere and by the end of the night, I ran out of the pub in terror, and got totally depressed. I mean totally depressed.

I believe that the body and mind were in a state of rejoicement at the addition of positive ions to them including the excellent energetic music of Fred enhancing the feeling, however, the combination of alcohol and claustrophobic surroundings, together with carcinogens, absolutely annihilated the feelings of euphoria. This then lead to the body and mind saying 'What the fuck are you doing man? Why the fuck do you go along and show us what life could be, and then rape it all from us again? Fuck you'

But I kind of feel grand agin now so I reckon that the negative energy vibe yeah man thing has totally dissipated.
Because positive energy is more powerful than negative energy when applied to life, yeah, dude, man, awesome........ of course it is. I think next Sunday I'll hit an island, please be sunny, please be sunny,
please Sun-God, shine down on me and deliver your radiance and energy onto my skin, I look to you for guidance in my hour of need. Please give me the strength to complete the task that lies ahead.
Yeah, I've decided to replace the lies of men with the truth of nature. God is alive, and it is all around you in the spirit of life........

I better go away now in fear that I shall be branded a heretic and cast out of this society for preaching the word of nature...... Hello boss, Nature is bad, Oil is good, Drink Oil not Water, motherfucker..........
aaaaaaaaaaaaaahhhhhhgggggggggggggrrrrrrrrrr
(Wincyscooderface)
wincyscooderface@yahoo.co.uk

POSTSCRIPT: Report from the World Social Forum, Porto Allegre, Brazil, January 2003, by former Charleville person.

"Tam, tam, tam - tamborez de paz", tambourines for peace, were words of a song sung by a choir in the Brazilan city of Porto Alegre, in the southern Brazilian state of Rio Grande de Sol. "Minha fulo me traz a meu tombar Me traz a meu tombar pra chamar Xongo . ." The choir, around twenty, dressed in white and singing like angles. They captivated the crowd in the Publico Mecado, the indoor Public Market, including me. Outside the streets swelled with colour and people. It was the March for Peace on the first day, 23rd of January 2003, of the World Social Forum which I had the privilege to attend.

Groups from all over the world gathered together in solidarity with the people of Iraq. I was bowled over the good will shown by everyone. South Koreans, Israelis, Mexicans, Bolivians, Drag Queens, Trade Unionists, Human Rights Activists, Europeans, Australians, Immigrants, US Americans, the list went on. Banners, colour, costumes, time and commitment - walking for a people thousands of miles away. I got a sense it was because they knew what suffering was like. I didn't.

This was the Third World Social Forum made up of thousands of non-governmental agencies and concerned people from all over the world. Over the next four days thousands of seminars, courses, discussions, workshops, theatres, exchanging of e-mails, personal testimonies, connections were to occur.

The next evening after attending conferences I saw the new elected President of Brazil Luis Inácio Lula da Silva, known simply as Lula address thousands of his fellow countrymen and women. He had been recently elected by two thirds of the population. He campaigned for a "decent Brasil",a decent Brazil for its people. His election victory was against wishes of the financial markets. The markets are seeking that Latin America put everything up for sale - water, land, foods, public education. Lula wants to put people first. The World Social Forum was set up as a counterpart to the World Economic Forum held each year in Davos. The former seeks the betterment of human beings across the world - "Another world is possible" is its slogan. What does the latter seek? Betterment of profits for capital no matter the cost? With the Enron affair should we all not be wary? At the

World Social Forum people are asking for basic economic rights - the right to education. Millions of children across the globe work as slave labour - the profit of their labour does not go to them. They are even denied the right to basic education. I am reminded of The Limerick Leader of the 1950s lambasting Ireland not providing free secondary education to its citizens. The State was content that they take up the lowest jobs abroad. Brazil emerged from military dictatorship less than twenty years ago. I witnessed the pride and hope of Brazilians in their President. There were rumours that president Hugo Chavez from Venezuela was there. Usually the World Social Forum invites the President of the host country and then no politicians or other heads of state are invited.

J Vincent, General Secretary of National Campaign on Dalit Human Rights from India was there. The Dalits are referred to as the Untouchable caste in India. In 2003 he and 200 millions others were seeking the basic right as being respected as fellow human beings. They live in segregated areas are daily humiliated. They cannot wear shoes and carry umbrella in the villages proper! He is just one of the people I met at Forum. I met an Amerindian whose grandfather was Portuguese buying a few books for his village in the Amazon Basin. Native Amerindians women working in other Latin American countries in the lowest paying jobs with little or no rights. I was informed of great role non-governmental organisations had in the setting up of the ban of Land Mines and of the setting up of the International Criminal Court. The Coalition for the ICC, a network of over one thousand civil society organisations from around the world, can be reached at - **www.iccnow.org**

At the Forum it struck me how Ireland is so lucky snug between the US and the UK. It did not become a pawn in the bitter Cold War. Also being white the effects of colonialism, the Famine excluded, were not as long lasting as elsewhere. Also because of the Land League reforms we were not exposed to the possibilty of a takeover by large corporate estate. The Land League and the Women's Land League, the non-governmental organisations of their time. I bought a book in Rio de Janeiro , "Poesia - Trdacao e Verao" by Brazilian translator and poet Abgar Renault. I found poems from Padraic Colum, James Stephens, Yeats, Cecil Day-Lewis, Oscar Wilde . Again it struck me how words, thoughts, ideas that cost nothing in money terms can survive, travel, contribute and transform.

The "Juvendade" was the Youth part of the World Social Forum. There were young people from all over the world. They had their own conference tent and also thronged the PUCAS, the Catholic University where most of the World Social Forum was held. The other main site for the Forum was in empty warehouse by the Lake- one warehouse for conferences on each of the Continents. Warehouse holding continents Asia, Europe, Africa, the Americas. Spaces let you bring your own table The camp site was beside the stage where Lula spoke, the stage on which for four nights the best of Latin Americas musicians and singers performed. The "Gigantinho". I attended the festival for three nights. People went through the crowd selling beer from containers carried on their shoulders. The beer was kept in ice cold water. There was no waste as others went around collecting the empty tins. In all the thousands of people I saw no one drunk. They definitely were a lot poorer than any Irish person at a similar concert. These people from countries are on the verge of bankruptcy, under pressure from outside banks, celebrating their culture, themselves, finding solidarity, looking for alternatives.

The racial mix at the Forum, at the Juvendade was staggering. How can you be racist if both grand fathers came from Europe, in the twentieth century migrations and your grandmothers two are Amerindians. What an artificial division race is - we are all human beings. The easy racial divisions just imploded As we all know racism is just an easy way to mark out others to fight against. If not race then something else. Any takers - religion, language, accent. A Brazilian asked me about skinheads in your country. Ah yes I said punks - Johnny Rotten, The Sex Pistols but he was talking about skinheads who beat up, hate and murder foreigners! I went to conferences on Human rights, on migrants,on the environment, on solidarity. I heard personal testimonies of people on the edge. I saw young theatre groups from the favellas (slums) of Sao Paulo. I saw a shaman perform a nature ceremony around a campfire beside a polluted lake. I talked to two Urguayan girls, Matilda and Lucai about culture and Oscar Wilde. I listened to all the music under the sun. I was stunned, the incredible wealth of people and cultures. Why not make globalisation work for people instead of markets.

When Jose Maria Figures, the managing director of the World Social Forum, was President of Costa Rica, INTEL set in that country. Did we convince INTEL to invest in Latin America by promising low wages workers, fiscal incentives or environmental concessions? The opposite is true he says. Cost Rica has the highest wages in Latin America, preferring to compete on the basis of higher productivity, not with hunger wages. Fiscal incentives are comparable to Ireland. He says globalisation will require us to harmonise taxes, raising them to adequately finance development. Costa Rica's environment regulation is comparable to that of developed countries. The destruction of a peoples' environment is a true disaster, I saw it in the Phillipines - let us hope the dumping of waste, body parts, illegally for the quick buck in Ireland is a thing of the past. Great Men for poisoning our drinking waters! On the last day of the conference I marched with a group of native Americans from Boliva, mesmerised by the music. In the World Social Forum I met people searching for solutions not only to their part of the world but to all the world. I met people with no economic power but with great humane and cultural power. The Anti War March on the 15th of February this year was endorsed by the World Social Forum. The next World Social Forum will be held in the city of Yderabad where the Asian Social Forum was held last year.

The World Social Forum, the World Economic Forum, I remember to other institutions with the word 'World' in them - the World Trade Centre, New York City that perished with many people from many nationalities so tragically lost. A despicable waste of life. I remember also The Church of the Cross Roads of the World by the bus depot in the same city. Why do I remember the image of crossroads? It was here I met Father Mychal Judge - another extraordinary and giving man, the first official victim of September 11th. The Church welcoming everyone, feeding the homeless. Father Mychal a son of Irish immigrants. I dare to suggest he saw New York as one of the Crossroads of the World, with thousand immigrants from the globe over going there each year. On the book he gave me he wrote "Érin go bragh! God Bless America!" May I add "Tudo Bem to the World!" "Um outro mundo é possíve", another world is possible. "Trazenda pro gente A paz mundial". To all at the NGO I went there with, keep up the good work!

appendix:

The third World Social Forum was quite literally a coming together of people in solidarity with other people. It is too big to describe in a few short pages. Here are some internet websites:

The World Social Forum Website is: **http://forumsocialmundial.org.br.**

The website of Transnational Institute, a non-governmental association is: **http: //www.tni.org**

A Social Water Forum is to be held in Japan from March 16 to 23. Website: **www.biodiversidadeglobal.org**

The World Education Forum was held just before the Social Forum. **Website: www.forummundialdeeducacao.com.br**

Ode Magazine website: **www.odemagazine.com**

Um Mundo Uma Luta - One World One Fight, supported by actionaid, the Ford Foundation and Oxfam. Website: **www.aoids2003.net**

The International Network for Economic, Social, and Culutral Rights can be found at **http://www.escr-net.org**

Amnesty International - **http://news.amnesty.org**

Féderation international federation des ligues driots de Homme, FIDH, (International Federation of Human Rights): **www.fidh.org/justice/index.htm**

(Discussions are currently underway on holding an Irish Social Forum in Dublin, some time this summer. Check internet for details)

Photograph by Deirdre Sheehan

165

The blank pages below are for all that which lies beyond the grasp of words or images, all that can't be expressed, all those who are in silence, all those who want and need silence. Do with them as you will. Leave them be, fill them up, tear them out.

index

Voices 2 CD compilation - music for the heart, head and soul

1. Sound-e-scape
2. Black Boys - Dragster
3. Everything We Had - Jamesie Foley and Friends
4. The Only Definite Thing - Jamesie Foley and Friends
5. Killybegs - Tommy Moogan
6. Quiet - Ultrahoney
7. Valentina - Ultrahoney
8. Creole Jazz - The Oscar Quartet
9. Bus Pass - Moonboot
10. Crowicide - Moonboot
11. Holy Hijacker - Moonboot
12. Antifun - Bandog
13. Saint Anthony - Bandog
14. Stars and Stripes - The Oscar Quartet
15. Starry Night - Michael O'Regan
16. September - Réidín & Shireen Russell
17. Trasna na dteannta (dul siar, dul siar) - Tommy Moogan
18. Taken By Surprise - Dragster
19. Pariah - Purgatory
20. I Will Return True - Pat O'Sullivan

All original music, copyright with the individual musicians. See p170 of Voices 2 for details.

information on tracks
tracks 2 & 18: Dragster(1977-1982) the Charleville band who, among many other things, came a famous second to U2 in a band competition in the Savoy in Limerick, were Billy Lynch(lyrics) - vocals/bass guitar, Pat Dempsey - drums, Pat Quealey - rhythm guitar, Joe Foley - lead guitar. Recorded circa 1979 @ Studio Fiona, Fermoy by Brian O'Reilly.
track 3: Jamesie Foley(words&music) - rhythm guitar, Connie Bowles - drums, Pat 'Chuck' O'Connor - lead guitar, Mark ?(Buttevant) - bass guitar. Recorded early 80s @ Studio Fiona, Fermoy by Brian O'Reilly.
track 4: Jamesie Foley(words&music) - vocals/guitar, Joe Foley bass/sax, Liam O'Sullivan - lead guitar. Recorded circa 1986 @ Studio Fiona, Fermoy by Brian O'Reilly.
tracks 5 & 17: Tommy Moogan - accordion. Recorded @ Effin, Feb. '03
tracks 6 & 7: Ultrahoney(1996-1997) were Mike Devine(lyrics) - vocals/guitar, Ray Murphy - drums, Sean Harrold - lead guitar, Dave Magner - bass guitar.

tracks 8 & 14: Recorded on January 19, 2003 @ Deerpark Hotel, Charleville. Jim Foley -clarinet/saxophone, Michael Murphy- drums, Jamesie Foley -guitar, Joe Foley - keyboards.

tracks 9, 10 & 11: Moonboot(1995-1997) musical adventurers, were Eddie Daly(lyrics) - vocals/guitar, Dave Magner - bass guitar, Ray Murphy - drums, Mark O'Connor - vocals/guitar.

tracks 12 & 13: Bandog (1999-2001) Limerick's alternative country outfit were Daniel Devine(lyrics) - vocals/guitar, Sean Harrold - guitar, Mike Devine - bass guitar, Ray Murphy - drums, Con Cremin - guitar.

track 15: Written, played & recorded by Michael O'Regan. Recorded Xmas 2002.

track 16: Copyright 2002 mammy music. Words & music by Réidín O'Flynn.

track 19: Purgatory, the latest assortment of Charleville-based lads threatening to musically break on through are Enda Buckley - rhythm/lead guitar, Ian Ryan(lyrics) - vocals, Denis O'Gorman - rhythm/bass guitar.

track 20: Patrick A. O'Sullivan(words&music) - vocals/guitar. Recorded @ Effin, Feb. '03. Pat, originally from Newtown, writes and musics his own songs, plays extensively on the continent and in Ireland.

Rock, traditional, ballad, jazz, metal, experimental... welcome to creativity, welcome sounds of love, emotion and freedom ... all different but all samples of creativity and all of/by people from this area.. local culture.. imagination.. and that's only an small subjective selection of what's out there. If some or all of this music sounds fresh, innovative and challenging to your ears.....that's because ... it is! And if you hear things you think you've never heard before, that's because .... you haven't! The older songs have held up well, the newer stuff shows that there are many people out there making real music. Music. Not combinations of sound, image, sex appeal, celebrity that generate money for the tv muck savages in designer suits. Long may they continue. This cd is an outlet for some of that music (that you never hear on the radio) and a document of local life.
Diversity of styles, diversity of creative and expressive urges.
These are broadcasts from local frequencies, so often blocked off by transmissions from above that we come to think that there's nothing happening here. Open up the airwaves.

Thanks to Seanín for the technical expertise to turn an idea into a reality, and Ray for saying 'go for it'.

"Evolution did not end with us growing thumbs. We're at the point now where we're going to have to evolve ideas. The reason the world's so fucked up is that we're undergoing evolution; and the reason our institutions, our traditional religions are all crumbling is because THEY'RE NO LONGER RELEVANT!!! They're no longer relevant! So it's time for us to create a new philosophy and perhaps even a new religion, and that's ok, because that's our right, because we are free children of God with minds that can imagine anything. That's kind of our role!"
from 'Rant in E-Minor' by Bill Hicks.